Creation

Presenting a brief and accessible overview of contemporary scientific thought, *Creation: From Nothing Until Now* is an imaginative and poetic exploration of our existence from an evolutionary perspective, from the Big Bang until now. The author assesses the religious and philosophical impact of scientific developments on our understanding of evolution and the natural world, and examines the changing relationship between us and our planet.

Willem B. Drees is a physicist, theologian and philosopher. He holds the chair in Philosophy of Religion and Ethics at the Department of Theology, University of Leiden, the Netherlands.

Creation

From Nothing Until Now

Willem B. Drees

London and New York

First published 2002 by Routledge
11 New Fetter Lane, London EC4P 4EE

Simultaneously published in the USA and Canada
by Routledge
29 West 35th Street, New York, NY 10001

Routledge is an imprint of the Taylor & Francis Group

© 2002 Willem B. Drees

Typeset in Sabon by Keystroke, Jacaranda Lodge, Wolverhampton
Printed and bound in Great Britain by TJ International Ltd, Padstow,
Cornwall

British Library Cataloguing in Publication Data
A catalogue record for this book is available from the British Library

Library of Congress Cataloging in Publication Data
Drees, Willem B., 1954–
    Creation : from nothing until now / Willem B. Drees.
        p. cm.
    1. Creation. 2. Religion and science. I. Title.
    BS651 .D75 2001
    213–dc21   2001019666

ISBN 0–415–25652–6 (hbk)
ISBN 0–415–25653–4 (pbk)

Contents

Introduction

Science

There is a great story to be told: the development of our world from the very first beginning up to our time, a history 'from nothing until now'. Through the sciences we have learned a lot about the natural history of our universe. Though our knowledge is neither complete nor final, some conclusions have been established beyond reasonable doubt. Hence, we have to take such scientific insights into account when we articulate and explicate our convictions. What does it mean for our view of humans, of human habits and culture, to know that we have come to be what we are via a long evolutionary process? What does it mean for our view of the Earth when we become aware that our planet is like a speck of dust in a huge universe – a universe that apparently once started small itself? This book is an expression of 'faith in the natural history of the universe', of confidence in our current view of the natural history of the universe – the history of stars and of life on Earth.

Creation stories

Humans have told each other stories for thousands of years. At campfires and in courts and temples, humans told stories about the origin of their world, of the hunting grounds of their tribe, of women and men, of the discovery of wheat and of fire, of the sun and the moon. Creation stories expressed how humans understood themselves in relation to their environment.

Such ancient myths are sometimes compared to scientific knowledge, as if the issue were factual correctness, say about a worldwide flood or about creation in seven days. When creation stories are judged in this way, they fail. When solely seen as factual claims, these narratives of a distant past are ready for the dustbin, or perhaps for a museum of cultural history. 'That is how people in the past thought about these things, but now we know better.'

However, creation stories can be appreciated as expressions of what moved people, what excited them, hurt them, made them feel grateful. In that sense, they go beyond the limitations of their own worldview. We can recognize them and identify with them, since we face similar challenges. Wonder about existence, awareness of dependence upon forces that are beyond our control, a sense of responsibility: these are themes that can and should be articulated as well in the language of our time. In that sense this book is not only an expression of confidence in the natural history of our universe, but also a quest for faith in the context of the natural history of our universe. How can we hold on to a humane sense of meaning, how can we articulate religious convictions in the context of what we know about our world 'from nothing until now'?

Narrative and justification

This book seeks to offer a justified creation story. It therefore is not just another popularization of science. We will reflect on our place and task in the light of the sciences. A first step in this project is the quest for new images. Poets may be better qualified for this task. Nonetheless I give my own wording of some aspects of the history of our world, a kind of 'creation story' – speaking of 'mystery', 'integrity', 'dependence' and 'responsibility' in an interpretation of the history of our world 'from nothing until now'. With such words, the story goes beyond the realm of science; it expresses a spirituality, a way of being in the world.

Images can be misleading. We should attempt to speak clearly and correctly. As I see it, the critical attitude of modern culture is a great gift. Thus, the larger part of this book is an explication and justification of this creation story. In the justification I relate to mainstream science as it has developed over the last few centuries. It is, in my view, not a good strategy to seek to save 'faith' by constructing a 'science' of one's own, as is done in fundamentalism (e.g. creationism) as well as by spiritual seekers (e.g. holism, astrology, parapsychology). Neither is it a good strategy to play down science too much. Science is not merely offering models that allow us to calculate the strength of a bridge. In my opinion, science is more than an instrument. With the theories and models of the last two centuries we are able to describe and explain very successfully large segments of reality. Through the sciences we are finding out about the way the world is.

We begin at the beginning, and thus consider ultimate questions – about the origin of our universe and its lawfulness (scenes 1–3). Then we will take a closer look at the development of the universe – the formation of matter and, on Earth, the emergence of purpose in a process driven by chance (scenes 4–6). One of the remarkable outcomes of this process, among many, has been the emergence of humans with their social and intellectual capacities, with morality and religions, and – a few centuries ago – with science and critical thinking (scenes 7–9). In three asides, I will consider the impact of modern developments on our understanding of the nature of religion, of science, and of reality.

We are the product of a long history, 'from nothing until now', as considered here. Time does not end with us; we are also producers. We are creative creatures. Thanks to the sciences and to our social organization, we have acquired enormous powers; we can modify our world. Thus, we need to become responsible beings (scene 10). The epilogue considers further our creative nature, both our involvement in changing our world and our freedom to develop new images and ideas about humans, the world, and God.

Environments

Humans are social beings. Those who came to hear me lecture on these issues have stimulated me to express myself more clearly. I am grateful to the board of the Nicolette Bruining Foundation for entrusting to me the Nicolette Bruining chair for philosophy of nature and of technology from a liberal Protestant perspective at Twente University, Enschede, the Netherlands (1995–2001). During the years this book took shape, I have also been enriched by faculty of the Vrije Universiteit in Amsterdam, especially by my immediate colleagues at its Bezinningscentrum, a centre dedicated to inter-disciplinary reflection on religious and ethical issues related to the sciences. Furthermore, I have benefited greatly from conversations with scholars and scientists from around the world.

As this book goes to the publisher, I am about to become Professor of Philosophy of Religion and of Ethics at the University of Leiden in the Netherlands. Predecessors in this chair have contributed in various ways over the last two centuries to religious thought which is responsible to its heritage and to contemporary scientific and historical knowledge. I also served as interim director for ALLEA, the federation of ALL European Academies. Academies of science and of scholarship in the humanities have always sought to recognize, promote and support academic quality and professional integrity. They also serve to communicate responsibly the best available science to policy makers and to the wider public. Even though the present book, with its mistakes, idiosyncrasies and biases, is fully my own responsibility, I hope that it may be an acceptable example of communicating scientific ideas and their potential significance.

The creation story was originally presented as one of the Andreas Idreos Lectures in May 1998, and subsequently published by Harris Manchester College in Oxford. Versions have also been presented at Northwestern College in Orange City, IA, Trinity College (Toronto), the University of Guelph, a workshop organized by the Ian Ramsey Centre at Oxford, and at Dartmouth College in Hanover, NH. Precursors were published in Dutch and in German. Elements of the following were also used in the Samuel Ferguson Lectures presented in May 1999 at the University of Manchester.

With gratitude I mention my wife Zwanet and my children, Johannes, Annelot and Esther. To these children, and to their friends of generations to come I dedicate this book. May the book inspire them to an open and responsible engagement with the wisdom that can be found in our religious heritage and with the knowledge uncovered by the sciences.

A creation story

There was a time
when there was no time,
when time was not yet.

The time
when there was no time
is a horizon of not knowing
a mist where our questions fade
and no echo returns.
Then,
in the beginning,
perhaps not the beginning,
in the first fraction of a second,
perhaps not the first fraction
of the first second,
our universe began
without us.

After the beginning,
perhaps not the beginning,
after the first fraction of a second,
perhaps not the first fraction
of the first second,
after our universe began,
still without us,
then
the universe was
like seething water
without land and without air,

like a fire
without wood and without cold.
The universe,
    as small as it was,
    created itself space, matter,
    and the cool of the day.

In billions of galaxies
    the universe made itself
    from dust stars
    from stars dust.
Much later,
    from dust from stars
    from dust
    from stars from dust
    swirled our Sun
    and from leftovers
    the Earth, our home.
Thus,
    after ten billion years,
    there was evening
    and there was morning:
    the first day.

Life
    a modest beginning,
    undirected,
    a history of failing
    and occasionally
    a small success.
A molecule
    carried information
    from generation to generation,
    history bred purpose,
    by chance.

Poison
    became a gift,
    oxygen
    a protective robe.

Billions of years later
    cells merge,
    sex and aging,
    death and deception.
A rare
    slow lungfish
    slithered through the grass;
    thus came amphibians to pass.
Successful life
    a disaster,
    gone
    another tide.

Yesterday
    a few million years ago
    the East Side Story:
    groups of apes groom,
    hunt and call.
Sticks, stones, fire
    eating from the tree of knowledge
    the tree of good and evil,
    power, freedom,
    responsibility:
Beasts became us
    more was delivered than ordered,
    more than we can bear?

Religion
    cement of the tribe
    response to power
    of mountains,
    the storm, the sea,
    birth and death,
    power as large as gods.
Yesterday
    ten thousand years ago
    Abel was killed by his brother,
    we farmers eat ashamed our bread,
    the earth cries, forever red?

A new age,
    a prophet warns
    king and people,
    a carpenter tells
    'a man
    who fell among robbers,
    was cared for
    by an enemy'.

Look,
    measure
    and count,
    challenge knowledge
    and authority!
Enlightenment
    way out of immaturity.

In us
    our heritage,
    matter,
    information,
    and a box
    full of stories.
Between
    hope and fear
    our neighbours
    life
    here on Earth,
between
    hope and fear
    the great project
    of thought
    and compassion
on a road
    of freedom.

Willem B. Drees

When time was not yet

There was a time
when there was no time,
when time was not yet.

Of old humans have seen the Sun and the Moon, the planets and the stars. The telescope, invented in 1608 in Middelburg in the Netherlands, revealed new details within our solar system, such as craters on the Moon and the moons of Jupiter. The telescope also enlarged our world: we came to live in a world of stars, with the Sun being one star among many.

A hundred years ago our horizon moved again further back: the stars that could be seen form together a galaxy, a disc with stars assembled in a few spiral arms. Our galaxy was not unique, but merely one of billions of galaxies, each with billions of stars. New technologies have moved the horizon back further and further. Each time we look further away, the universe turns out to be larger than previously thought.

In 1676 Ole Rømer measured the velocity of light by checking carefully when the moons of Jupiter passed the planet in front or on the far side. He concluded that light travels at a finite speed. The speed of light, about 300,000 kilometres per second, is a huge velocity for us, but so are distances in the universe. Light from the Sun takes eight minutes to reach the Earth. Light from the next nearest star takes a few years.

On 23 February 1987 astronomers saw the explosion of a star in a nearby galaxy, the Great Magellanic Cloud. Old news – the explosion had taken place about 200,000 years ago. Light from other galaxies takes even longer. Current technology allows us to notice objects so distant that light has taken billions of years to reach us: we see the universe as it was in the past.

An eternal universe?

Is there a limit? Or will we always look further away, and thus also farther back in time? How far we can see depends on our technology. But is there in principle a limit, or will there be ever more galaxies, beyond any horizon?

It is now thought that one cannot always look further away. To support this idea, one does not need a telescope; it is enough to be aware that it is dark at night. Imagine that one is in a forest. Some trees are nearby; others further away. We are close to one tree, which blocks our sight in that direction. If it is a small forest, with not too many trees, we might be able to see through the forest to the open field. But in a large forest one will not be able to see beyond the forest; in all directions one will see trees. Similarly in a universe: if it were filled with galaxies and if it were sufficiently large, galaxies would have been in our line of sight in all directions. Stars would have been in our sight in all directions. Hence, the sky should be as bright as the surface of a star. Day and night the sky should be as bright as the Sun. But it is dark at night. Hence, the universe cannot be filled with stars until infinity. This argument arose at the end of the seventeenth century. It is called Olbers's paradox. Every night the darkness proves that the universe cannot be infinitely old and infinitely extended.

The Big Bang theory confirms this view of the universe. On the basis of observations and well-tested theories cosmology has made a reconstruction of the history of our universe. This history encompasses about fifteen thousand million years. The figure is not very precise, since it is hard to be sure about distances in the universe. However, whether it is twelve or twenty billion years, current know-ledge is that the universe with all the galaxies we see began billions of years ago and has been expanding since. In later sections, we will come back to the development of the universe. Here we will reflect on this notion of a 'beginning'.

A beginning in time?

One might think of the beginning of the universe as one thinks about the beginning of a work of art. At some moment *in* time it was made.

Time may be imagined as the ticking of a clock, an infinite extension of moments. At one of those moments my life started, over a thousand million seconds ago. Long before that the Earth was formed. At again an earlier moment, some fifteen thousand million (10^9) years ago, the universe began.

If it started at some point in time, what preceded the universe? This question arises naturally upon such an approach. Before the work of art, there were the artist and her materials. Before my conception there were my parents. What was there before the universe?

This question was already raised in a different form in antiquity. Augustine, one of the major theologians in early Christianity, around 400 CE discussed the question what God was doing before God created the world. If you see creation as the beginning of the world, what was the Eternal One doing that infinity of ages before there was a world? Augustine first makes a joke, effectively saying: 'Then God created Hell for those who ask such questions.' But then, Augustine attempts to deal seriously with this question.

Augustine argues that the question is wrongly posed. The question what God was doing *before* creating the world, assumes that one can meaningfully speak about 'before' even when there is no world. This assumes that time is unrelated to the existence of a world. But time is connected to movement: the pendulum of a clock, the rotation of the Earth, the frequency of an atomic oscillation. If there is no clock ticking and no Earth rotating, how could we then say that time passes? Time assumes movement and hence matter. Augustine understands time, to use religious terms, as an aspect of creation and not as an attribute of God. If earth and heaven are not there yet, time is a meaningless notion. Augustine thus concludes: 'If there was no time before heaven and earth, why then ask what Thou were doing then? For when there is no time, there is no "then".'

A beginning of time?

Augustine rejected the idea of creation *in* time; time was something that came into being *with* creation. This is the kind of solution that contemporary cosmologists are seeking as well when they develop theories about the universe as a whole. Time is a notion that is related to material processes. In the very early universe, processes were different, and hence the notion of time was too. Perhaps, 'time' is not a well-defined notion when we approach 'the beginning of time'. Rather than a sharp boundary, a moment when the initial push was given, there may perhaps have been a twilight, like the transition between day and night.

It may be that reality was different then. Or the problem may be ours, due to our inability to describe the situation well. Stephen Hawking, a cosmologist, uses the image of the north pole as an analogy. Everywhere on Earth one can point 'north'. Except when standing on the north pole; there all directions are 'south' (or 'up' and 'down', but 'above our heads' is not what we mean by 'north'). On traditional maps, the north pole is not a point but a line, the upper boundary of the map. Nonetheless, the north pole is a regular point on Earth – there too the horizon is around us in all directions. The Earth is slightly curved, just as everywhere else. It is our concept 'north' which is useless there. Hawking argues that 'time' is no longer a useful concept when we seek to describe the early universe. That is not a tragedy, nor does it suggest that there is 'another side'. Rather, it is a limitation of our language. A concept that is useful for many purposes need not be applicable everywhere.

There are various other views. They all wrestle with the concept 'time'. This is not a problem in ordinary life. The problems arise when one extrapolates back, in the context of the Big Bang model, until about 0.000 000 000 000 000 000 000 000 000 000 000 000 1 second from the (apparent) beginning. The image has been that the Big Bang model describes our universe as expanding from an initial state of infinite density and temperature. However, this model is only reliable to the extent that the physical theories

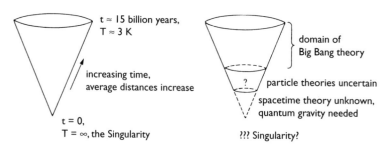

Figure 1 On the left the Big Bang model is depicted as a cone, with each horizontal slice representing the three-dimensional universe at a given moment of time. On the right the major uncertainties are stressed.

Note: (t stands for time; T for temperature)

assumed are well developed and tested in the laboratory. Cosmologists are just like historians or archaeologists who seek to understand the past. They go backwards from our time and place, and somewhere will enter less well-charted terrain. The closer we get to the initial state, the more this is the case. In that sense, the Big Bang theory is not about the Big Bang, but about the development of the universe since a slightly later moment.

To extend the domain further, theories about matter (quantum physics) and about space, time and gravity (general relativity theory) have to be integrated. Such an integration has not been achieved yet, though there are various ideas and proposals. Some speculative theories describe a universe with an ultimate boundary; other ideas suggest that our universe has arisen out of a different, 'preceding' reality. Such ideas are hard to test. We cannot recreate in a lab the conditions of the very early universe, but these ideas can be tested to some extent; a good theory should explain the development of our universe.

Perhaps the boundary of our knowledge will be moved further back. Perhaps almost all these speculations will turn out to be untenable within a few decades, with only one generally accepted theory about the first fraction of a second remaining. The way it seems to be now, paradoxical as it sounds, is that we have to do with 'a time when time was not yet', a phase of the universe when our notion of 'time' was not applicable. And if 'time' was not yet applicable, we are confronted with a beginning that was perhaps not the beginning, a first fraction of a second, which perhaps should not be called the first fraction of a second.

Though the new understanding of time would be forged in order to grasp 'the beginning', the ensuing understanding of reality would apply at all moments – and thus affect deep down our understanding of time and history. Cosmology challenges us to explore alternative views of time and reality, and thereby to free ourselves from a way of thinking which comes so naturally to us, namely the view that everything happens in time.

Scene 2

Mystery

> *The time*
>> *when there was no time*
>> *is a horizon of not knowing*
>> *a mist where our questions fade*
>> *and no echo returns.*
>
> *Then,*
>> *in the beginning,*
>> *perhaps not the beginning,*
>> *in the first fraction of a second,*
>> *perhaps not the first fraction*
>> *of the first second,*
>> *our universe began*
>> *without us.*

Will we ever be able to answer all questions concerning the early universe? The way I see it, science will be able to move back the horizon. We will see further, and hence differently. Our horizon might shift, but I believe that science will not remove this 'horizon of not knowing'. There will always be 'a mist where our questions fade, and no echo returns'.

A creation story begins with the beginning, but we do not know our reality as a film shown to us from the first scene onwards. Our situation resembles the predicament of archaeologists. We find traces and clues – and seek to understand the past. In that process, we answer questions and pass on other questions.

An architect who designs a building decides to use concrete. He has, we hope, knowledge of the forces that this concrete will be able to withstand. If someone would ask why the forces are as they are, the architect might refer us to an engineer who studies material sciences. This engineer should be able to inform us about experiments and the relevant theory, about the wear and tear of the materials concerned, and their relations to chemical bonds between the various materials. Perhaps the engineer even knows from which geological deposit the sand and cement have been taken. However, if you go on asking how those layers came to be there, the engineer will refer to a geologist. The geologist can tell a story about the erosion of mountains and sedimentation of sand and stones by rivers. Perhaps the geologist can discover that the sand used was part of a particular mountain range, and perhaps even that the same material was already deposited on a sea floor before. However, if one continues by asking where the silicon and oxygen come from, the chemical elements making up sand, the geologist will have to say that these were there when the Earth formed. For further questions, he will refer to the astrophysicist. And the astrophysicist can answer many questions, about the formation of elements out of hydrogen in the interiors of stars and during supernova explosions, and the way these elements are distributed in the universe and may get included when a solar system forms (see scene 4). However, this explanation assumes that there is already hydrogen as the material out of which stars are formed. When we go on with 'historical' questions we come to theories about the earliest stages of the universe, to the turf of the cosmologist.

This, in a nutshell, is typical of science. Scientists answer questions belonging to their province of expertise, while passing on other questions, about the things they take for granted in their own work. In the end, two types of questions remain. There are persistent questions about fundamental rules: Why does matter behave the way it actually behaves? Why are the laws of nature the way they are? What is matter? There are also persistent questions of an historical kind: Where does everything come from? How did it all begin? Such questions arise again and again when a sequence of questions is pursued. They are questions at the boundaries of science, 'the horizon of not knowing'. Scientists can explain much, but that does not get one around these questions. The horizon moves, but is not removed.

Some people have attempted to answer such questions in a different way, by referring to our own existence. If we had not been there, we could not pose such questions. The universe is as it is, since that is the kind of universe in which we can exist. If the universe had been slightly different, life as we know it could not have come into existence.

That life would not have come into existence in a universe which was different seems to follow from various thought experiments. If one makes a mathematical model, one can also see how the universe would have developed if certain conditions and parameters had been different. What if the universe had slightly larger mass, or a slightly higher velocity at the onset of the expansion? What if the electron were a tiny bit heavier than the actual one? An electrical force which is smaller, or stronger compared to gravity? Why not space with two dimensions rather than three? And so on. All kinds of variations can be tried in our models. Such modifications, even small ones, can be shown to have major consequences, at least in the context of such models.

An example. The universe as we know it seems much larger than we need for our kind of life. We do not need much more than a solar system. And if we want to be generous, one galaxy with some hundred billion stars is large enough for us. Could the universe, then, not have been much smaller? The size of the universe seems pointless, wastefully abundant for a creator interested in life, and especially in conscious and responsible life such as humans. But is the size really pointless? If there is to be enough time for the formation of the heavy elements (see scene 4) and for the evolution of life (see scenes 5 and 6), the universe has to exist long enough – but then it also has to be large enough, since the longer the universe exists, the further light has travelled. Also, in order to be big, the universe needs sufficient mass. According to current scientific models, a universe with the mass of a single galaxy would expand for only one month before collapsing again. Life could not have developed.

Let us assume that our universe is indeed 'just right' for our kind of life. Does that have a deeper meaning, for instance a conscious choice picking those conditions that allow for humans? Does this provide a clue for faith in a creator intending humans to be?

In discussions on the universe there has been talk of 'anthropic principles'. The choice of terminology is problematic, for it is not specifically about a universe in which humans (Greek: *anthropoi*) can exist, but about a universe in which a planet such as ours with the right kind of materials has sufficient time to bring forth life through evolution. Thus, it might be more appropriate to speak of a 'biotic principle' rather than of an 'anthropic principle'.

Besides, humans also experience all kinds of misfortunes in this universe. A classic example is the buttered toast falling upon the floor with the buttered side down. A colloquial expression for the pessimistic mood is Murphy's Law: If things can go wrong, they will. Careful analysis shows that the same conditions which allow for the emergence of human life, which optimists have appealed to in speaking of 'anthropic principles', are also those that make buttered toast fall from human tables upside down. Thus, perhaps there is an 'anthropomurphic principle' at work.

Upon closer inspection, we are not dealing with a well-defined 'principle', but rather with the realization that there might be a mix of circumstances hospitable to us. Thus, one might speak of 'biotic coincidences'. The question then is what significance might be attached to those biotic coincidences.

Perhaps it is a matter of selective observation. If we were to live in a train and look out of the window, we would notice that railroad barriers are always closed. What a pity for those that stand waiting there; those cars will never get across. That is of course nonsense; we see closed barriers since we look at the world from within the train. That the conditions in our part of the universe are just right for us could be a claim of a similar kind, a consequence of selective observation. Where and when the conditions are different, we will not be and hence we will not observe such regions.

Another possibility is that coincidences that seem as if they could have been different, will be shown to be a consequence of a further developed theory. Since the discussion on 'anthropic coincidences' emerged, this has happened already to some extent. A new model was proposed, the inflationary universe. According to this model, the early universe went through a phase of extremely fast expansion. This model skilfully combines standard insights about matter and the Big Bang theory, and explains some features which are otherwise arbitrary, such as the homogeneity of matter and radiation in the observable universe – a feature previously explained by appealing to an 'anthropic principle'.

Thus, even with respect to properties of the universe our puzzlement and our current questions may well be answered by future theories. At the same time, new questions emerge in the context of new theories. For instance, the inflationary model does not explain why the universe is such that inflation happens; some assumptions are always made. The reach of explanation is impressive, but explanatory successes do not exclude further questions. Again and again, questions emerge at the limits of scientific understanding.

Questions remain even if physics and cosmology agree one day on a complete theory, a theory explaining all known phenomena in a unified, coherent way. Imagine, a single article, a single formula answering all our questions. But the article is on a piece of paper; the formula consists of symbols. Thus, there is no answer to the question: Why does reality behave as described here? It is as with a drawing by the Belgian artist René Magritte. It is a careful drawing of a pipe, a pipe used for smoking tobacco. Underneath it, he has written 'Ceci n'est pas une pipe' – 'This is not a pipe'; and he is right. It is an image of a pipe. One cannot fill the image with tobacco, and attempting to light the image would have a very different outcome from lighting a pipe. There is a difference between an image, however accurate it may be, and reality. This is also the case for a good scientific theory. However accurate the theory, the question remains why reality behaves as it does (and as described in the theory).

There is a traditional philosophical question: Why is there something rather than nothing? There are similar philosophical questions that arise due to science, but are not answered by science. Why is mathematics so effective in describing reality? Why is reality such that we can work well with wrong, or at least incomplete theories? For this is our predicament, since we do not have a theory integrating quantum physics, gravity and space-time. It is a mistake to inflate problems and puzzles to mysteries, which would perhaps only be open to a religious answer. Such an approach would be forced into further retreats again and again. However, the success of science in solving puzzles and problems can itself evoke questions. Why is science so successful? What does that say about humans and about reality?

There are various ways of dealing with such persistent questions. It is said that the American president Harry Truman had a sign on his desk saying 'The buck stops here'. In a company or administration one can pass on hard decisions to persons higher up, but the president cannot avoid responsibility; he has to make a choice. Scientists, however, do not have to make a choice. They have to live with the insecurity of unanswered questions. A political decision or dogmatic answer is neither necessary nor adequate. Religious people do not have to cut this Gordian knot either. They ought to be willing to recognize that our explanatory quest is open ended. The physicist Charles Misner expressed this well: 'Saying that God created the universe does not explain either God or the Universe, but it keeps our consciousness alive to mysteries of awesome majesty that we might otherwise ignore, and that deserve our respect.' Perhaps we will never come to a final explanation. We always work within the limitations of our concepts and ideas and within the limitations of our existence. We never see the universe 'from outside', from the perspective of eternity, but always from within. That is also a problem when we speak of God; we are within the universe while we attempt to speak about something more encompassing. Our language about a 'beyond' need not be meaningless, but our theology does require agnostic restraint if we are not to fall into an arrogant and unwarranted religious certainty.

The more we know, the more we may become aware of the limitations of our knowledge. *De docta ignorantia* (About learned ignorance) was the title of a book of Nicolas of Cusa, a cardinal in Europe in the fifteenth century. The scientific road to knowledge has shown itself to be very successful; we have learned more than Nicolas of Cusa and his contemporaries might ever have expected, but that does not need to result in the arrogant conviction that we can explain everything without any residue. On the contrary; through science we are confronted with fundamental questions concerning the nature and ground of our reality. Why is there a reality? Why is reality the way it is? Thunder is no longer a voice of the gods, nor is it a mystery, but that does not exclude wonder regarding the reality of which both we and the thunderstorms are part. On the contrary, in the end existence remains a mystery.

Scene 3

Integrity

After the beginning,
perhaps not the beginning,
after the first fraction of a second,
perhaps not the first fraction
of the first second,
after our universe began,
still without us,
then
the universe was
like seething water
without land and without air,
like a fire
without wood and without cold.
The universe,
as small as it was,
created itself space, matter,
and the cool of the day.

There always will remain questions; existence does not explain itself ('mystery', see p. 18). However, if we only stress the inexplicable, we would lose sight of the integrity of the universe, the reliability of phenomena. It is not as if something unexpected and incomprehensible can happen any moment. Rather the contrary; the universe in its development turns out to behave according to regularities (laws of nature). If the universe is seen as a gift, the present is a complete one; it has its own integrity. It is not a puppet on a string, with someone else pulling the ropes, or an incomplete product that needs supplementation or correction from time to time.

In earlier times, this seemed different. Newton's theory of gravity explained the movements of the planets in our solar system, but not completely. The system seemed to run off the track from time to time, needing a special act from the creator to keep it on course. The French mathematician Pierre Simon Laplace (1749–1827) showed that the deviations did not accumulate disastrously. This is captured well in the following anecdote, of which the historical veracity is doubtful. Laplace presented a copy of his book on the movements of the planets to Napoleon. Napoleon is said to have remarked that Newton in his treatise referred to God, whereas Laplace did not do so. Upon which Laplace is supposed to have replied: 'Your Majesty, I do not need that hypothesis.'

Indeed, contemporary cosmology does not need a God-of-the-gaps. In that sense, the situation is quite far removed from ordinary experience. When we maintain a fire, we need to supply it continuously with new wood, and we need an environment that is cooler than the fire – an environment to which the fire gives of its heat. The universe seems to do without such input and without such a receptive environment – a fire without wood and without cold; it creates itself space, matter, and the cool of the day.

That there is no need for the difference between the hot fire and the cold night is just one instance of the very fundamental issue of asymmetry arising out of symmetry. In the physics of ancient Greeks such as Aristotle, the Earth was at the centre, a very special place. Heavy objects 'by nature' fell to the centre; that was their 'natural place'. Over time, we have become more modest with respect to our own position. Neither the Earth, nor the Sun, nor our Galaxy is the centre. There is no centre. There is no cosmic discrimination of this kind; all places are equal. At least, equal in principle. In practice, places can be extremely different – from the hot interior of the Sun to the extreme cold of intergalactic space.

When there is no discrimination – with respect to place, time, orientation, or otherwise – physicists speak of symmetry. Newton's law of gravity did away with the concept of 'natural place', and thus with discrimination by place – masses such as the Moon and the Earth attract each other, depending on their distance, but where in space this couple would be makes no difference. Discerning symmetries has been a very powerful technique in physics, since symmetries are closely related to the existence of conserved quantities. If processes are not sensitive to place, there is a conserved quantity, momentum (velocity × mass). If processes do not discriminate with respect to time – an experiment being performed today or tomorrow is expected to produce the same results – there is another conserved quantity, energy. Theories in fundamental physics are characterized by the symmetries that are built into them.

Symmetries can be spoilt. In the language used by physicists, symmetries can be broken; and they have been broken. Think of traffic. In principle, there is no reason why driving on the right or on the left hand side of the road would be preferable. If you are the only one driving around, it is attractive to keep to the middle of the road. However, once there are more cars around, the symmetrical solution (driving in the middle) becomes unattractive. If some drivers agree to drive on the right side of the road, others will follow, since the asymmetrical pattern is more viable than the symmetrical one. What triggers the choice may be minute. Indonesia was for many years a Dutch colony – and the Dutch drive on the right-hand side of the roads. However, the first car bought by the Sultan was a British Rolls Royce. Thus, driving on the left became the rule in Indonesia. To understand how a symmetry has been broken, we need history. Contingent facts may make a huge difference.

In the perspective of physicists, the fundamental rules of the universe have many symmetries built into them, even though the universe has become a world with many particular features which spoil those underlying symmetries. In biology, it is often the other way round; the symmetry is in the product, but not in the underlying process. For instance, the human body appears to be symmetrical with respect to left and right. However, underlying this appearance, there are all kinds of asymmetries, with respect to the heart, with respect to control over fine hand movements, and deeper down with respect to the way fundamental molecules are structured in space.

Now let us forget about life on Earth for the moment, and concentrate on the universe as it starts to develop. The early universe was homogeneous, whereas we nowadays distinguish cold and hot places, e.g. the night sky and the Sun. Through the expansion of space, the universe cooled. Clumps of matter, formed by gravity, generated hot spots. Thus, matter and gravitational contraction fuel the fire, while the expansion of space allows the fire to radiate away its heat.

We may not need to provide the universe with hot places and a cold environment, but we do seem to need matter to make our universe be what it is. However, according to modern cosmologists, for our universe it is not necessary at all to have an explicit input of mass or energy 'in the beginning'. This is amazing, since we see a lot of matter around us – the ink and paper of this book, our bodies, the house we are in, the Earth, the Sun and all those stars – that cannot be just nothing?

For physicists, it is all mass, and mass is a form of energy. Energy can take the form of movement, heat, and mass. Something can also have energy since you have lifted it; when one drops a stone, that energy is released again. Some objects may have a negative energy; it takes energy to bring a stone up from the basement to ground level. It also takes energy to launch a rocket into outer space, to free the rocket from the Earth's gravitational attraction. It takes even more energy to launch a rocket so that it escapes the solar system. And we need again more energy to free a rocket from our Galaxy. How much energy would be needed to launch a rocket that not only escapes from the Earth, the Solar System and the Galaxy, but even from the universe? That requires a lot of energy. It may take all the mass-energy that the rocket represents. But once the whole rocket is used as fuel to overcome the negative gravitational energy of the universe, there is nothing left to escape – the net energy of the rocket may be zero.

This thought experiment can also be used in reverse. Perhaps our universe is, as far as energy is concerned, 'nothing'. There is an enormous amount of mass (which is equivalent to a huge amount of energy), but that mass is subject to gravitational forces – and this implies an enormous amount of negative energy as well. The same applies to electrical charge. When there is a thunderstorm the clouds and the surface of the Earth have a different electric charge, but taken as a whole the system may well be neutral. The universe needs no input of charge, mass or energy; the conserved sums might be zero.

This self-sufficiency does not imply that nothing is needed. For a thunderstorm to arise, positive and negative charges must become spatially separated out of a neutral whole. The emergence of a material universe presupposes a reality in which matter can form out of energy. Quantum physics describes that process. According to this theory, there may be a fluctuation during which two opposites form, for instance a positive and a negative charge. Empty space is like a seething ocean, with waves rising and falling. After matter has formed, the universe is still like a seething sea in which combinations of matter form and fall apart.

If matter forms in space, then where does space come from? If we find ourselves in an expanding universe, as the Big Bang theory has it, should there not be an environment into which the universe expands? Space seems to be an external, pre-existing resource made available to the universe continuously.

Cosmologists have given an amazing answer to questions concerning the origin of space. The universe expands, and thereby creates its own space. The image of the Big Bang as an explosion, with bits and pieces flying apart, is misleading. There is no centre nor an environment in which the pieces move.

Let me try to explain this with an example. A balloon with dots is inflated. An ant on the surface, near one of the dots, sees all the other dots moving away. And the further away another dot is, the faster it recedes. However, the ant's dot is not the centre of the dots; from the point of view of any dot, all others recede. If we only pay attention to the surface of the balloon, we have an analogy for the cosmological case – the surface expands, but not by adding new material. Space (the surface) itself is stretched. The dots do not move over the surface (nor the galaxies through space), but they move with the surface. The inflation of the balloon shows itself in the increasing distances between the dots, just as the expansion of the universe shows itself in the increasing distances between galaxies. Perhaps a cake with raisins might be a three-dimensional analogy for the two-dimensional surface of the balloon – from the perspective of any raisin, all the other raisins seem to be moving away as the cake rises during baking.

It is hard to imagine, but according to current theories the universe may have created its own space. With the expansion of the universe it cooled down (except for hot spots like the Sun). Temperature differences, including the decreasing temperature of outer space, drive the formation of structures that would not have been stable at higher temperatures.

The universe has its own integrity; it stands on its own feet, without a supply of mass, energy or space flowing in from elsewhere. We speak of 'laws of nature' describing the development of the universe. These laws are the invariant elements in our descriptions; they are what holds everywhere, always. There is no dictator who occasionally brushes his own laws aside and decides otherwise. No shifts from the automatic pilot to manual control. No miraculous interventions. The universe develops itself; it has integrity.

Responses to this integrity of reality are different. Some see it as a basis for atheism, the conviction that there is no God. This interpretation passes silently by the limit questions considered above (see scene 2). The integrity of the universe does not imply that everything is understood; it is something other than self-sufficiency.

Others see the integrity as a basis for deism, the idea that a god started the universe but is not involved in it anymore. However, fundamental limit questions are not only questions about the beginning; they are also questions about existence and lawfulness. The question why the universe is as it currently is, is not answered merely by saying that this is so now since it was yesterday as it was yesterday. It is also necessary that the laws of nature are effective *at every moment*, that reality has existence at every moment.

As long as we speak in terms of cause and effect, we assume the ordinary notions of time and space. God can be thought of as the creator of the first moment; then and there the fuse was lit. However, since space and time are difficult concepts when we speak of the universe as a whole (see scene 1), we can and should distance ourselves from the image of God as an engineer who started the whole business. In the theological tradition God has been referred to as the 'First Cause', who is the cause of the 'secondary causes', that is, of natural processes and natural laws. Perhaps we should take even more licence from our concepts of time, space and cause. In this context, I prefer to think of God as the sustaining Ground of Being who is also the ground of the natural order and its integrity. To use an image from the novelist John Fowles, one might perhaps say that like the silence that contains a sonata and the white paper that contains a drawing, God sustains our existence. God would be considered as a sense of potentiality, of non-existing, a 'dimension in and by which all other dimensions exist'.

Scene 4

Dependence

In billions of galaxies
  the universe made itself
  from dust stars
  from stars dust.
Much later,
  from dust from stars
  from dust
  from stars from dust
  swirled our Sun
  and from leftovers
  the Earth, our home.
Thus,
  after ten billion years,
  there was evening
  and there was morning:
  the first day.

After some ten billion years, two-thirds of the history of the universe so far, the Earth and the Sun formed. As far as the Earth is concerned, it was not until then that there is a first day. If we are interested in a religious or secular view of our own lives, those first ten billion years without days may seem dull and unimportant. The utmost limit we already have discussed in the preceding scenes, while humans and human cultures are not to appear on the scene for a long time. However, by paying attention to this long period without humans we may become aware of the extent of our dependence upon the larger universe in which we live, move and have our being.

In the first few minutes of its existence – speaking in terms of the Big Bang model – the universe was as hot as the inside of stars. New nuclei formed and broke apart. At the end of those 'first three minutes' ordinary matter in our universe consisted mainly of electrons, protons (becoming the nuclei of hydrogen atoms) and the nuclei of a few of the lighter elements, especially helium. A few hundred thousand years later the temperature had dropped sufficiently for the next big step; out of nuclei and electrons hydrogen and helium atoms formed. Then the universe became transparent; light was no longer scattered continuously by matter.

Matter was distributed very homogeneously. However, there must have been some clumpiness, some minor inhomogeneities. The description and explanation of those is one of the most active areas of research in cosmology. The presence of such inhomogeneities is important. Small concentrations of matter attract more matter, and thereby become the beginnings of (groups of) galaxies.

Within a galaxy there are huge clouds of hydrogen. Gravity makes such a cloud collapse. After millions of years, a dense ball of gas forms. The temperature rises and nuclear fusion takes off. Through this process energy is released – a star is born. The star does not collapse any further; nuclear energy provides enough pressure to withstand gravity.

A star can be understood, unromantically, as a nuclear fusion reactor, merely kept together by gravity. In the core of a star like the Sun, nuclei of hydrogen fuse and form helium with a mass equivalent to four hydrogen nuclei. In our Sun, this process will be going on for about ten billion years; the Sun is about halfway through this life cycle. In bigger stars the temperature and density inside is higher and the transmutation faster.

When the available hydrogen in the core has been used, the energy production stops, the pressure thus generated falls away, and the star will continue its gravitational collapse. In consequence, the density and temperature rise even further. Under these circumstances, helium nuclei will merge, resulting in heavier elements such as carbon and oxygen. This process too releases energy. The star will settle in a stable state for a time, until the supply of helium has been exhausted. After a further collapse (and increasing density and temperature), new fusion processes will take off. In this way, heavier elements such as carbon, oxygen, and phosphorus are formed inside stars until the process results in iron. Further fusion would not produce energy; rather, for heavier nuclei (such as uranium) fission releases energy.

When the 'fuel' inside stars has been converted from hydrogen to heavier elements, the star will collapse under its own weight. This generates a huge amount of heat, resulting in an explosion. For a few weeks the star will burn very brightly, as if there is a very bright new star in the heavens – this is called a supernova. During the explosion the heavier (and rarer) elements such as gold, lead and uranium are formed. In the explosion, the outer layers of the stars are blown away. The remnant may be a dwarf star. If there is enough mass left, it may also become a very dense neutron star, or even a black hole, a concentration of mass so compact that not even light can escape its gravitational pull.

We humans have a special interest in the dust blown away during such explosions. The explosion injects the elements formed inside the star into the interstellar gas. While only hydrogen and helium formed during the first few minutes of the universe, the interstellar gas thus came to contain traces of other elements. These are included in stars of the second generation, which also form from interstellar clouds. These second generation stars at the end of their career further enrich the interstellar plasma.

Our Sun is a star of a later generation. In 1814 the German optician Joseph Fraunhofer made a spectrum of the light of the Sun. (A spectrum is an image in which the different colours, from red to violet, are spread out as the colours of the rainbow.) Fraunhofer discovered dark bands in the spectrum of the Sun. Every set of lines relates to a particular element. In this way, scientists in the nineteenth century discovered that the Sun contains iron, calcium, magnesium, sodium, nickel and chrome. In 1868 an unknown element was discovered in the spectrum of the Sun; it was named 'helium'. In 1895 it was isolated on Earth.

Traces of heavier elements, produced in earlier generations of stars, can be found in the spectrum of the Sun. These elements also form the basis of the planets, including Earth, and they are the basis for all life on Earth, since life is dependent upon carbon, oxygen, phosphorus and much more. All these elements have been formed through nuclear fusion in earlier stars. The only exception are the hydrogen atoms, present for instance in water. For the other elements we owe our existence to the perishing of stars we have never seen. We are not just dust of the earth (Genesis 2:7), but dust from stars from dust from stars from dust. Gratitude might well extend beyond our parents and grandparents to include even the stars that burned long before the Sun began to shine.

Scene 5

Purpose

> *Life*
> > *a modest beginning,*
> > *undirected,*
> > *a history of failing*
> > *and occasionally*
> > *a small success.*
> *A molecule*
> > *carried information*
> > *from generation to generation,*
> > *history bred purpose,*
> > *by chance.*

At the end of the nineteenth century Mark Twain used one of the marvels of technology to articulate the significance of humanity.

> Man has been here 30,000 years. That it took a hundred million years to prepare the world for him is proof that that is what it was done for. I suppose it is. I dunno. If the Eiffel Tower were now representing the world's age, the skin of the paint on the pinnacle knob at its summit would represent man's share of that age, and anybody would perceive that the skin was what the tower was built for. I reckon they would, I dunno.

The time scale of life on Earth is now thought of as even more grandiose than it was by Mark Twain, but that makes the sense of disproportion even more prominent: the time of humanity is like the skin of paint on the knob at the top of the Eiffel Tower. Knowledge of natural history diminishes the cosmic significance of human existence.

From a biological point of view the purpose of evolution is not humanity, nor is it diversity, complexity or intelligence. Evolution happens, without a purpose. Within the evolutionary process, however, purposiveness has emerged. For the eye *is for* seeing and the kidneys *are for* filtering blood. These organs have a purpose, a function. How can one think of this remarkable feature of our history from nothing until now, that purposiveness has emerged in a process without purpose?

As long as reality is considered only at the level of cause and effect, as in physics and chemistry, there is no place for function, let alone purpose. Events happen as they happen. That is the point of departure of the evolutionary developments: events happen. Mutations, small changes in the features of organisms happen. Among the mutations some may be helpful while many others are disastrous – helpful or disastrous for such an organism in such an environment. The environment is a source of accidental events too: one organism may find useful food, whereas the other starves; one gets eaten, the other escapes. Accidents are selective; some organisms make it, whereas others do not. Here too there is no goal-directedness; the environment is not selecting for a particular development.

The combination of accidental mutations and accidents in life results in more than accidental development. Subsequent generations will have properties that are slightly better in tune with the hazards of that environment. Natural selection by the environment is not aimed at any particular purpose (as humans may be when breeding dogs or roses), but natural selection does make differences. Individuals that happen to have somewhat more suitable properties will on the average and in the long run do better than others who have slightly less attractive properties. The properties at stake can be various: resistance to drought, alertness, sharper claws, a longer stem so that more light is captured, or a restriction to bare essentials, as in duckweed. Those individuals that happen to be better equipped for their environment will have, on the average, more descendants than less well-equipped individuals of the same kind. Features that are advantageous for the life of individuals will thus, in the long run, be on the rise in the history of life.

Purposiveness is a consequence of such history. A tree has a long trunk *because* that allows the tree to capture more light. (In passing: Are tree huggers and tree lovers aware of the asocial nature of trees with their impressive trunks? Trees try to capture as much light as possible, to the disadvantage of fellow plants.) A rabbit has eyes on the side *because* this allows her to see early any predators approaching. Why-questions can properly be asked when we have to do with life that is a product of history. Organs have a purpose; they serve an important function and developed in the way they did since similar organs fulfilled that function reasonably well in previous generations.

Purposiveness in individual organisms arose through non-purposive evolution, by history in which information was passed on from generation to generation. This history is the basis for our abilities but also for our limitations. We never make a clean start. We are tied to our history. An example is the human eye, an organ that fulfils its purpose (seeing, which is itself instrumental for all kinds of further purposes such as gathering food, selecting mates, reading animal tracks and books) very well. However, the nerves that come from the cells of the retina depart on the front side. As a bundle they pass through the retina to the brain. This creates a 'blind spot'. We are so used to our blind spot that we do not notice it, unless we try in a particular way. The arrangement with nerves first going out to the front side also makes us vulnerable to a detached retina. A pragmatic engineer would have done the wiring differently; the output of signals could be wired from the back. However, once the eye has evolved in this way, it is not likely that evolution will ever stumble upon the better solution. To reach that pinnacle, we would have to get down from our somewhat lower pinnacle and pass through a valley of less effective designs. There is no anticipation, no foresight that allows the process to take a less advantageous route for a couple of generations since that will be more advantageous further down the line.

Nor is there any anticipation with respect to grand scale changes. Dinosaurs may have been very well adapted to their environment, and the evolutionary design may have been flexible enough to accommodate small changes in the course of generations. However, they were not prepared for the impact of a comet and the consequences of that impact for the climate on Earth. Evolution shows no foresight. Even more than at other moments major catastrophes make it a matter of chance and luck who will carry on the banner of life.

Neither perfection nor anticipation of changing circumstances is a direct fruit of evolutionary processes. However, in the course of biological history there is an accumulation of 'ideas' about effective living, passed on as information embodied in the DNA. Such a cumulative history thus marks the transition from a world of cause and effect to one of purposes, a world of physics and chemistry to a world that also needs biology to be understood. Evolution generates purpose, but does so through a long sequence of chance events.

Scene 6

Luck

Poison
    became a gift,
oxygen
    a protective robe.
Billions of years later
    cells merge,
    sex and aging,
    death and deception.
A rare
    slow lungfish
    slithered through the grass;
    thus came amphibians to pass.
Successful life
    a disaster,
    gone
    another tide.

The Earth formed about 4.5 billion years ago. There was no atmosphere with oxygen then. Nor was there an ozone layer high in the atmosphere. This is, seen from our interests, a huge disadvantage, since the ozone layer filters most of the destructive ultraviolet light. Oxygen and ozone in the atmosphere arose in history; awareness of this history confirms our dependence on processes that occurred long before we were born.

In the beginning the Sun was less brilliant than it is now. The Earth was cold; water must have been frozen most of the time. An atmosphere of carbon dioxide and nitrogen formed. This worked as a blanket; it generated a greenhouse effect. The Earth retained more heat and the temperature rose. Ice melted and the first oceans developed. Carbon dioxide dissolves reasonably well in water. Rain, rivers and oceans absorbed carbon dioxide from the air, and deposited it as limestone. This undid part of the greenhouse effect, just when the brilliance of the Sun was increasing, so that the Earth did not retain too much heat.

Our nearest neighbour, the planet Venus, went through a similar process, except that the temperature was slightly higher. Oceans did not form; the water evaporated and contributed to the atmosphere. The greenhouse effect escalated even further when the Sun became more brilliant. Venus now is a planet with a very dense atmosphere (the pressure at the surface is about one thousand times the pressure on Earth) and a hot surface.

We were lucky with the temperature. We had good luck with oxygen too. Oxygen is an aggressive gas. It makes iron rust, and also corrodes other materials. If there had been free oxygen in the early atmosphere, the first complex molecules would have fallen apart quickly. Whether life could have evolved is very dubious. Oxygen came into the atmosphere not until much later, through one-celled algae who developed photosynthesis. They captured energy from the Sun; oxygen was for them a poisonous waste product. For a long time the oxygen they released was captured by the oxidation of iron ore and other minerals. Some two billion years ago the oxygen level in the atmosphere started to rise significantly, reaching its current level 1.5 billion years ago. Because of the presence of oxygen some organisms developed a different metabolism, which was more efficient than the earlier anaerobic metabolisms. However, there still are single-celled organisms that neither use oxygen nor could survive its presence in their environment. Some such bacteria live near hot springs in oceans; others inside us.

Oxygen made a more efficient metabolism possible. It had other consequences as well. Out of oxygen (O_2) ozone (O_3) formed in the atmosphere, filtering ultraviolet light. Water also filters UV; life would have been restricted mostly to the water if not for the ozone layer. However, thanks to the ozone life on land became an option. With the protective ozone layer and the more efficient metabolism, it became feasible to be a multicellular organism moving around on the land.

The atmosphere is a gift. But the atmosphere has – to run ahead of our story – also become a task, a responsibility. We humans make a dramatic impact on major systems of our globe. We generate changes more quickly than the changes due to non-human causes.

Consequences of our activities are not obvious, since there are so many interacting mechanisms, some accelerating or at least confirming a trend, others compensating through a negative feedback. We are dependent upon the gift of the atmosphere and have the responsibility, for our children and grandchildren, but also for all other forms of life on Earth, to slow down human induced changes to make the biological consequences more manageable.

When we speak of life, we tend to think of animals such as cats and lions, birds and fish. Trees and flowering plants are also important in our appreciation of nature. However, for billions of years there were only single-celled organisms. Some 3.5 billion years ago the bacteria and, as a different form of life, the archae-bacteria developed. Within the world of single-celled organisms the variety is enormous. The genetic difference between different types of bacteria can be greater than the genetic distance between a human and a plant.

Some 2.5 billion years ago the eukaryotes formed, single-cell organisms which are in volume typically ten thousand times the size of the prokaryotes. They have their genetic material stored in a well-defined core. They also have small 'organs' with their own function, as units within the cell. Perhaps such organelles are descendants from independent cells, now in a symbiotic development within the eukaryotic cells. Perhaps the symbiosis should be seen in a more unfriendly light, as genetic material has moved from mitochondria and other organelles to the core – thereby robbing the organelles of their independence. One author spoke in an article in the *Scientific American* even of a 'progressive enslavement of the captured endo-symbiont prisoners by their phagocytic [cell-eating] hosts'. However one judges the balance of power within the eukaryotic cell, this new partnership is a major step in evolutionary history, comparable to the emergence of the first cells and of multicellular existence. One additional transition of major consequence must have been the evolutionary development of photosynthesis leading to cyano-bacteria (prokaryotes). By inclusion of such bacteria into eukaryotic cells, this history resulted in brown, red and green algae – the last of these giving rise to green plants.

Within the eukaryotic stream multicellular life emerged a billion years ago – plants, animals and fungi. With multicellular organisms complexity increased. Then too sexual reproduction began, the combination of genetic material from two parents as the basis for a new individual in the next generation. Bacteria and other single-cell organisms reproduce by division, producing two similar descendants out of a single parent cell. This makes a difference with respect to death. With sexual reproduction the new individual, a child, is clearly distinct from each of the parents. Parents grow old while the evolutionary lineage continues with new individuals. With cell division in bacteria this is less clear; the cell divides but there is no direct analogy of aging and dying. Bacteria can be destroyed, for instance by heating and by antibiotics, but they do not age. With multicellular organisms the existential problems that occupy humans truly began: sex, aging and death.

How obvious is the result of evolution? If we assume that we would have a similar initial situation on another planet, would we see the same development? Or, to use another metaphor, if we would run the same experiment again, would we see the same sequence of events? Would evolution result again in intelligent living beings such as ourselves who baptized, modestly, our own species *homo sapiens sapiens*, the very wise human? Did natural history run a similar course on planets near other stars? Are there similar intelligent and moral beings elsewhere in the universe?

A first step in answering such questions concerning the *contingency* of our existence is to consider whether there are planets that provide a fertile basis for life. Planets are dark and small, compared to their star. This makes them hard to detect. Nonetheless there have been various claims during the last few years about the discovery of planets. In some cases the period, mass and distance to the main star have been determined. It may be quite likely that there are in our universe planets in abundance. They seem to form as a side product with the formation of a star out of dust.

Would life emerge again on a suitable planet? On Earth the first forms of primitive life formed early, within a few hundred million years after the crust formed. Is that typical? In August 1996 there were claims that simple, single-celled forms of life had once existed on Mars. In a meteorite found in Antarctica some organic materials were found (polycyclical aromatic hydrocarbons) such as we find on Earth in oil, coal and barbecued meat. A product of bacteria? It was suggested that there might be microfossils in the meteorites, one ten-thousandth of a millimetre long. The meteorite seems to be from Mars, ejected when an asteroid made an impact on Mars, some fifteen million years ago. That the meteorite has its origin on Mars is fairly generally accepted among the relevant specialists. However, the interpretation of the evidence as indicating life on Mars has been heavily disputed. Sceptics argue that there may well have been 'pollution' from Earth, picked up during the thirteen thousand years that this meteorite has been in Antarctica, 'waiting to be found'. The microfossils are so much smaller than even the smallest bacteria on Earth, that it is very questionable to interpret them as cells. Extreme miniaturization has been a late development in human technologies such as electronics; it seems likely that that is the case for evolutionary developments in nature too. Even if – a very major if – the meteorite is evidence of organic life on Mars, would this life have emerged independently from such life on Earth? For a cross fertilization between Mars and the Earth may have taken place before as well. If – IF! – the organic Martian origin would be credible, this meteorite would be the first proof of life elsewhere in the universe, but such strong claims require strong evidence.

The claimed discovery drew a lot of attention in newspapers and on television. This is helpful in generating funding for space exploration. However, public attention was not limited to mini-bacteria of a ten-thousandth of a millimetre. Cartoons and editorial comments jumped almost immediately to advanced, intelligent life. Intelligent extraterrestrials populate many movies for children and adults. If life has begun somewhere, how likely is it that we will move beyond single-celled organisms to higher, more complex forms of life? Apparently, this did not happen on Mars, even if a start were there.

The specialist in fossils Stephen J. Gould considers it extremely unlikely that history would ever produce a similar result. Even if we were to start a million times again, it still is improbable that beings like humans would emerge again. Gould takes his point of departure in the beginning of the Cambrium, a geological period when life had already become multicellular. In a particular formation of rocks in Canada, the Burgess Shale, fossils from this period, some 530 million years ago, have been found. Among them Gould claims to discern twenty-five different forms of life, each of which could have resulted in a particular kind of animals, such as the insects or the vertebrates. Only four of those twenty-five still have descendants. If some others had survived, life would be quite different now.

Gould points to many other transitions when it could have been different. Among the vertebrates there was a small and insignificant group of lungfish with bones in their fins allowing them to move on the land; if they had not been there, the vertebrates might have never been able to invade the land.

If at the end of the Cretaceous period, some 65 million years ago, the impact of a meteorite or comet had not led to the extinction of the dinosaurs (except for the ancestors of birds) they might still dominate the Earth; a more extensive form of consciousness might not have developed. Dinosaurs were a successful form of life; a disaster and it was over, with new opportunities for other life forms. Not astrologically but biologically we owe our existence to the positions of the planets.

Again another happy accident: If among the primates in Africa there had not emerged a few million years ago a species with an upright posture, despite their interesting potential the primates might have been restricted to ecologically marginal species such as the chimpanzee, the bonobo (sometimes misnamed dwarf chimpanzee) and the gorilla. The human species, *homo sapiens sapiens*, is according to Gould

> a tiny twig on an improbable branch of a contingent limb on a fortunate tree.

The accidental character of any evolutionary development is not the consequence of a fundamental process, as perhaps in quantum physics, or of the randomness of genetic mutations. Rather, the issue is the coming together of different, independent chains of cause and effect. We consider it luck that we meet someone on the street and thereby may collect a debt, even if we both have good reasons to be there. The current outcome of evolution is the result of many consecutive steps, each one intelligible but in their multitude and variety as a whole unpredictable.

The accidental, contingent character of evolutionary history can be disputed. Gould's interpretation of the Burgess Shale has been challenged substantially in a careful study by the palaeontologist Simon Conway Morris, who has worked extensively on the fossils of the Burgess Shale. Perhaps convergence in relation to the constraints of existence is a major characteristic of evolutionary processes. It is not accidental that mammals such as dolphins have a similar shape as fish and as extinct marine reptiles (ichthyosaurs) – this shape is well adapted to the challenges of moving effectively in the seas. A practical solution may be discovered more than once.

On Earth flying has been invited a few times, by insects, flying dinosaurs, birds and mammals (bats). In the animal kingdom eyes have been invented at least forty times. Those eyes are different in construction but functionally to a large extent equivalent, helpful in finding food and in avoiding becoming food. Hence, it is not unreasonable to expect that such a sense organ would have evolved even if natural history had been somewhat different, and that 'eyes' would emerge on other planets if there were multicellular 'animal' life and 'light' to benefit from.

That good tricks have been invented more than once does not speak for but rather against the idea that a human-type intelligence is a frequent product of evolution. Such a higher form of intelligence arose only once among the billions of species, even if more restricted forms of intelligence seem to have evolved also outside of the vertebrates, among the octopuses. If one of the many switches had been in a different position, would our form of conscious life never have come into existence?

There are many stars, some hundred million per galaxy; and there are many galaxies, some hundred million in the observable universe. Even if evolution would find the road to intelligence only rarely, it may have found it elsewhere in this huge universe nonetheless. However, it is not likely that this happened 'just around the corner' since the emergence of intelligence is too accidental. Hence, I consider it very unlikely that we will receive signals from intelligent beings in our cosmic neighbourhood, say within a hundred or thousand lightyears – and even at such relatively close distances, 'communication' will be extremely slow. Even less likely are encounters with extraterrestrial aliens; reports about contacts with and abductions by aliens reveal more about human imagination and mass psychology than about life elsewhere in our universe.

Sometimes people are frightened by the enormous contingency of our existence, which, by the way, is also there at the level of our immediate origins – our grandparents meeting and mating, and then our parents meeting and mating, and this particular combination of egg and sperm coming together. However, in my opinion, the contingent, accidental nature of our existence does not diminish its value. Rather to the contrary, the contingency of our existence makes it something special, not easily reproduced. Humans arose in the course of biological evolution. Consciousness, playing with ideas and reflecting upon our own activities, has risen to a level not present on Earth before. That life and consciousness arose in material beings through a long historical process does not diminish their value; rather, such amazing consequences should raise our esteem for the potential of matter. The contingent character of the process is also a basis for freedom and responsibility, for it affirms the role of small local influences on the course of events; the future is not fixed in an unavoidable process, by laws determined, but rather the product of history as it is made by creatures such as us.

Humanity

Yesterday
    a few million years ago
    the East Side Story:
    groups of apes groom,
    hunt and call.
Sticks, stones, fire
    eating from the tree of knowledge
    the tree of good and evil,
    power, freedom,
    responsibility:
Beasts became us
    more was delivered than ordered,
    more than we can bear?

The Rise and Fall of the Third Chimpanzee is a book about humans. We are so close to the chimpanzee and the bonobo that the label 'third chimpanzee' is to the point. But there are also major differences. The other primates are almost extinct whereas humans with their languages, their science and technology dominate the Earth. How did we arise in the course of evolution? What can we learn from our own history?

On these issues various details and some essentials are disputed. The evidence is incomplete. Sometimes we do not even know whether the pieces are of the same puzzle or whether we are mixing up fossil remains of different lineages. But the uncertainty is no reason to avoid facing our own history as far as reconstructed now.

Within the superfamily of the monkeys some thirty million years ago the family of the apes formed. This family currently includes the gibbons, the orang-outangs, the gorillas, the chimpanzees, bonobos and humans. The study of our living relatives, and especially of our second cousins the chimpanzees and the bonobos, may throw more light on human nature. However the significance of the results should not be overestimated. For instance, among chimpanzees males are dominant; many conflicts are resolved by fighting or threatening. This has led many scientists and anthropologists to the conclusion that the social dominance of males among humans is given naturally. Status is dependent upon the threat of, or willingness to resort to violence. However, among our equally close cousins the bonobos (sometimes called dwarf chimpanzees) social relations are shaped differently. Females are dominant. Conflicts are more often resolved by sex than by violence. Hence, a univocal lesson about 'human nature' cannot be drawn easily from comparisons with these other primates.

The East Side Story: the evolution of anatomically modern humans

We might also learn from the history by which modern humans arose since the last ancestors we shared with the chimpanzees. Some five million years ago the lineage leading to humans and those leading to chimpanzees and bonobos separated. Fossils and finds from the period thereafter do not yet indicate big brains, an upright posture, or the 'cultural' ability to make tools. Small teeth with thick enamel seems a distinguishing feature, indicating a diverse diet, and thus, perhaps, beings who could adapt to different circumstances.

Some 2.5 million years ago the climate cooled. In Africa west of the Great Rift Valley, where some of the great African lakes are, the rainforest persisted. On the East Side of the Rift Valley, the rainforest gave way to grass. The East Side Story is an essential part of our history. The savanna required adaptations. From this period various fossils have been found, both of individuals of a heavier build ('robust') and more 'gracile' ones. Different species emerged. On the basis of fossils researchers distinguish, among many other types, *paranthropus robustus*, *paranthropus boisei* and *australopithecus africanus*, and also *homo habilis*. For life on the savanna upright walking and hunting in groups may have been beneficial. The oldest stone tools seem to date from this period, from Hadar in Ethiopia some 2.6 million years ago.

Other lineages have become extinct. In the homo lineage standing and walking erect developed further. Some 1.8 million years ago *homo erectus* spread from Africa across Europe and Asia. Individuals of this species developed a bifacial axe with curved surfaces and sharp blades (the Acheulian culture). They also used fire. The ability to control fire indicates a further rise in mental and social capacities.

The next big step was the emergence of *homo sapiens* out of *homo erectus*, one or two hundred thousand years ago. Is this a development which took place in one group, once in Africa, with the new species spreading from there across Africa, Europe and Asia, replacing the earlier *homo erectus*? If the theory is right, Africa was at least twice central to the emergence of modern humans. Or did *homo erectus* develop further in different places, with the emergence of a new species, *homo sapiens*, stabilized via mutual exchange?

In discussions on the evolution of humans most attention has been given to Africa. However, Europe and Asia may have contributed to the transition of *homo erectus* to *homo sapiens* as well, as William Calvin, a neurologist, suggests in *The Ascent of Mind*. The fourfold increase of our brains, compared to chimpanzees, started about 2.5 million years ago, coinciding with a series of ice ages. During those ice ages, which lasted tens of thousands of years, there were remarkable changes that happened relatively fast. When the climate became more attractive a population explosion could take place, especially among those who lived on the border of the ice-covered areas since they had access to new territories as the ice retreated. The next ice age would move the frontier of habitable territory south again, and thus our ancestors too. Through those migrations genetic and cultural adaptations emerging in arctic or moderate climates merged into the heritage of all hominids.

In moderate and cold climates these groups will have depended upon hunting, unlike warmer areas where one might expect to find fruits and seeds. Hence, a 'northern' adaptation could have been the ability to throw with precision. A fast movement such as throwing an axe (which perhaps was more a frisbee than an axe) needs the coordination of various muscles, a coordination which has to be done in advance since correction once the arm has started its swing is only feasible for slow movements. This advance coordination might have been a factor in the emergence of language as an ordered sequence of words.

Whatever the precise story of the emergence of *homo sapiens*, we came to be. There were at least two subspecies of *homo sapiens* in

Europe, namely *homo sapiens sapiens* and *homo sapiens neanderthaliensis*, until some forty thousand years ago. Cro-Magnon humans, our ancestors (belonging to *homo sapiens sapiens*) created artful images of animals on rocks as well as many useful tools. Their culture is called Aurignacian culture. Judged by the artifacts they were capable of abstract thinking and they appreciated beauty. They may have had religious sensibilities as well, since they buried their dead in special ways, with gifts in the grave.

The other subspecies, 'Neanderthaler', is often depicted with apish looks, but they too had their culture; Mousterian culture. If we look at their culture with the same criteria in mind we may perhaps conclude that they too had a sense of beauty and the ability to use abstract thought. They too buried their dead with rituals, and exhibited highly developed social behaviour. At La Chapelle aux Saints remnants have been found of a man who had lived to a relatively old age, about thirty years, despite the fact that he must have been severely handicapped during his life.

Neanderthalers have disappeared. What happened to them is not yet clear. Perhaps they were replaced and extinguished by *homo sapiens sapiens*. Perhaps they were integrated, absorbed into that group.

To summarize: The emergence of modern humans has gone through many stages, with a variety of lineages, of which in the end only one persisted. Hominid evolution may have started with the ability to adapt feeding habits to a variety of environments, followed by upright walking and the use of tools (*homo habilis*). Mental abilities increased further with the use of fire and perhaps the use of relatively well coordinated movements in hunting (*homo erectus*). Relatively recent is the emergence of cultures with more extensive ritual and social behaviour (*homo sapiens*). It is this social and cultural behaviour that seems to make us special.

The evolution of moral culture

Humans have come into being through an evolutionary process. Most of us have no objection to this being applied to the loss of fur, but it is more sensitive when we consider spiritual matters, such as morality. Would an evolved morality be really moral? How could morality ever come to be through evolution, since my moral behaviour benefits others rather than me or my own children?

Social behaviour towards children, nephews and nieces is evolutionary intelligible as a form of genetic 'self-interest' (and thus not fully deserving the epithet 'moral'). Genes that promote social behaviour in the family promote the spread of copies of themselves in the next generation. Support of one's partner is also evolutionary intelligible, since the shared investment in children results in common interests. For beings with a reasonable memory, helping one's neighbour is also evolutionary intelligible. After all, another time I may request help from my neighbour.

Helping a stranger may perhaps be understood as an example of 'indirect reciprocity'. By displaying social behaviour my status in the group may rise, and indirectly this may result in pay-off. There may also be explanations in terms of the interest of the group (tribe, village). By doing something for the group my group may thrive in comparison with competing groups. Hence, my children will benefit as well. We may benefit even more when we invest less in the common cause than it appears, since then we profit in the benefits that befall our group without sharing the burden to the full extent. The evolution of deception is, upon this view, intertwined with the evolution of social behaviour. There is not a definitive evolutionary explanation of the rise of social behaviour and of the habit of evaluating the behaviour of others in moral terms, but the various ideas together may do the job quite well.

Is moral behaviour less valuable when it is evolutionary intelligible? Dishonest, not genuine? We withdraw our hand from a flame. Those who did not do so, became handicapped or suffered from infections. Hence, they produced children less often or were less able to protect and support them. But upon the question 'Why do you withdraw your hand?' the answer is not 'In order to have more children', but 'because it hurts'. That the sensitivity to pain and the reflex of withdrawing have evolutionary explanations does not make the pain less real. This also applies to morality: the existence of an evolutionary explanation for pro-social behaviour does not imply that we are not driven by genuine moral considerations and sentiments. Rather, moral sentiments are the means by which a fruitful social life has become possible.

When humans oppose each other some are said to behave 'beastly'. Based upon an evolutionary view, is not all our morality 'beastly' in origin? Our moral principles seem to be nothing but the form acquired by our natural intuitions and emotions, our preferences and dislikes. Can we distance ourselves from patterns of responding that formed during the Stone Age with its glacial periods, if not before among apes in the trees of Africa? We have been gifted with considerable intellectual power invested in smart weapons and strategies; is that more than we can handle morally?

'More was delivered than ordered'. Means can be used for new purposes. The fingers did not evolve to play a piano, but they can be used to play the piano. In evolutionary history new uses of old organs can be found again and again. Intelligence and communication, brains and language will have been useful for the four essential F's: feeding, fighting, fleeing and reproducing. Once intelligence and language evolved, they may have been used in other tasks as well. In that sense, evolution again and again delivers 'more than was ordered'.

The 'more' that was delivered allows morality to be genuinely moral. For our intelligence allows us to reconsider our own behaviour. We may, for instance, discover that we are 'naturally' inclined to treat men and women differently. However, by becoming aware of this we can also act against the apparently self-evident 'natural'. Communication may also contribute. Imagine that once an offended hominid asked a fellow hominid: 'Why do you behave thus?' The one who is challenged could not just appeal to self-interest or emotions ('I just like to do this'). In the presence of others he or she was challenged to justify the behaviour in question with arguments that would be recognizable and acceptable to the others – and thus, to formulate some general principles justifying his or her behaviour. In many incidents of this kind, natural behaviour guided by enlightened self-interest may have become reconsidered, intentional behaviour. The social context of our lives may have pushed towards universality and accountability, hallmarks of morality.

We have been equipped with intuitions and emotions. That is already a mix of nature and culture. Furthermore, we are occasionally open to reason, to argument. Since ideas spread faster than genes (which are transferred only to one's own offspring), culture may develop enormously. There is no reason to assume that the biological basis would always overrule the effects of culture. Thanks to the emergence of culture as a second kind of heritage, alongside the genetic one, and thanks to the capacity for reflection and to the impulse to public justification, we are not victims of our evolutionary heritage. We are biological beings, but as these particular biological beings we have a moderate amount of freedom with respect to our genetic drives. We therefore also have responsibility.

Material thinking

An evolutionary approach challenges our self-image in many ways. We are biological beings. We are also nothing but material beings. In the scientific understanding that informs our culture, including our medical practices, there is no immaterial ghost in the machine, no soul that departs at death. We are psychosomatic unities, that is, bodies that display mental behaviour. Chemicals such as those in coffee, wine and Prozac influence our mood. And reverse: ideas, beliefs and desires influence our bodies.

Regarding humans as material beings challenges our self-image. Material processes go their way; they are not 'about' anything. The sounds we utter and the markings we scribble on paper are 'about something' – we write about love, we do arithmetic, we put down on paper how to prepare an apple pie.

If thinking is just a complex chemical and electrical process going on in our bloody brains, why would it be different from digestion which goes on in our bowels? What would be left of the content of thinking, the truth and significance of words, ideas and symbols? If the conclusion of the scientific view of the world would be that bloody brains do not produce meaningful ideas, but merely be complex chemical processes that produce noises mistaken for meaningful words, we would be caught in a paradoxical situation – since science itself is one of the activities which assumes that we are engaging ideas, not merely noise.

The sceptical attitude seems to follow from the idea that all the work in brains is done by chemical processes. It may be that the current state of the brain corresponds to a particular state of mind, but the next state of mind is merely the byproduct of the way the brain will be in a second from now, and that is a matter of circuits and neurotransmitters, not of ideas. Thus, if you are thinking about '23 + 47', and say '70', you would not say 70 because of the mathematics, but because of the way the brain is wired. The picture seems to be as follows:

Mind	'23 + 47'		'70'
	↑		↑
Material state	Brain at t_1	→	Brain at t_2

All the work seems done at the lower level, by the physical processes, with no real contribution from the meaning of the ideas. However, in writing this book, in you reading this book, we are engaged in an exchange of ideas. At least, that is what we are striving for. Thus, an extremely reductionist view of human personhood seems insufficient; ideas are more than an irrelevant byproduct of the material processes. We seem to need a ghost in the machine. The scientific picture is essentially incomplete, unable to account for human nature.

This pessimistic conclusion arises due to neglecting specifics of the horizontal arrow, which indicates the complex physiological process between hearing '23 + 47' and answering '70'. This process is a material process, but it is not just any process. We give the answer we give because we have been trained to make precisely those connections, from the time we started to learn words and numbers. There is a lot of content involved in the horizontal arrow, the nature of our thinking – years of training, recollection of other experiences, and so on.

One could make a similar analysis of computers. Under one description, there is nothing but a physical process going on, with electric charges and magnetic states changing. Using this description, there is no reason at all to believe that a computer gives the correct answer to the question '23 + 47'. If it were to answer '69', there would also have been a complex process occurring in the chips of the computer. Physics would still hold. However, we expect the computer to reply '70' because that is the right answer. With computers we have started to use a second level of description, describing it as a machine that deals with numbers and ideas. The crux is that engineers have designed the computer in such a way that our expectations regarding the way numbers and ideas are managed correspond to the physical processes executed. Some years ago there was a problem with a Pentium chip; certain calculations went astray. There was nothing wrong with mathematics, the world of ideas. There was nothing wrong with physics – the electrons behaved according to the laws of nature. The correspondence between the two – between the world of material processes and the meaning we ascribed to the symbols involved – was not constructed as it should have been.

Whether by design or by learning, 'matter' (we, bodily beings) can think adequately. This is not degrading humans; rather, it is upgrading our view of matter. We humans are biological beings; we have brains – but it is precisely by being constituted thus, that we can deal with content without paying attention to the underlying material processes. However, we are fallible in this; if we make mistakes, we will start to consider the underlying process. Have I heard you correctly? Or, if it is a more persistent problem, do I really know the meaning of those words? Or, if the problem is more severe, we sometimes have to conclude that the organization is damaged by a tumour or a stroke, incapacitating the processes we relied upon.

Reductionism has a bad press. However, if we acknowledge that 'higher' phenomena are rooted in processes at a lower level, the reality of the 'higher phenomena' is not denied. Reduction implies the contrary: the reduced phenomenon is real. Pain remains painful, even if at a different level of description pain is identified with certain nerves giving signals to the brain. If I go to see my doctor and she explains the processes that generate my pain, I am not embarrassed. To the contrary, when I come home I can say that my pain is real; I am not faking. Water remains water, even when its chemical composition is understood to be H_2O. Reductionism is not a denial, but a form of integration, of understanding how various phenomena are part of a larger whole.

As a challenge to a religious understanding, a reductionist integration need not be as threatening as is often thought. Would it be a problem if God has created a reality with one basic kind of stuff, rather than a reality with two (bodies and souls) or with ninety-six kinds of stuff? In the scientific understanding of phenomena in terms of underlying processes, we learn more about the coherence and potential of our reality. We are no exceptions to our world, no outsiders, but beings who exemplify some of the rich potential of reality.

Scene 8

Religion

Religion
  cement of the tribe
  response to power
  of mountains,
  the storm, the sea,
  birth and death,
  power as large as gods.
Yesterday
  ten thousand years ago
  Abel was killed by his brother,
  we farmers eat ashamed our bread,
  the earth cries, forever red?
A new age,
  a prophet warns
  king and people,
  a carpenter tells
  'a man
  who fell among robbers,
  was cared for
  by an enemy'.

Religions arose in human history. The evidence is indirect. Whereas fossils may reveal an upright posture or a particular brain size, convictions do not leave univocal traces. Graves may provide clues. Ritual burial was already an established practice tens of thousands of years ago, even among the Neanderthalers. Perhaps they believed in an afterlife.

Religions need not be seen as merely by-products of human evolution. Rituals and myths may have been essential in the emergence of humans. Genetic and cultural information co-evolved in our evolutionary history. The more culture demands, the more brain capacity becomes an important asset for those endowed with it. Culture is a social phenomenon, present in groups of hominids. Living together must have been a serious challenge. Among the ants the social life of large groups is supported by the genetic relatedness between the individuals involved. Among hominids this has not been the case, at least not to the same extent. How did groups manage to live together? Myths and rituals may have been essential as cement of the tribe. The rituals that make the boy into the warrior and the girl into the bride, affirm everybody's place in and commitment to the group. Myths, stories transfer the values of the group from generation to generation. Without such religious support for social order humans would not have evolved in the way they have.

Religions also emerged in confrontation with the power of storms, of the sea and the mountains, thunder and lightning. When confronted with unpredictable events we still use animistic language. We even do so in our dealings with technological products; the car 'does not want' to start and the computer 'does not understand us'. Animistic language seems outdated, a projection; lightning is no longer seen as thrown down upon us by wrathful gods. But still we humans use such figures of speech, though often in more positive versions as talking with trees, discerning 'a plan' in life's events and denying meaningless contingency.

Religions may have emerged partially in the confrontation with the accidental in our own lives and those of others dear to us. One can think, also in our time, of transitions and crises such as birth and death. Religious language is, among other things, a way of speaking of humans who have to cope with aspects of reality they do not understand or control. Thus, religious practices and beliefs may have been important to our ancestors as ways to maintain social, cosmic, and personal order.

Agriculture began about ten thousand years ago. Humans crowded together in small areas such as fertile plains along rivers. This gave more opportunity for small elites to control the harvest; societies became more hierarchical. There will have been conflicts between sedentary farmers and nomads with their cattle. In the Hebrew bible, the Old Testament, we see traces of such conflicts. The nomadic sons of Jacob travel for food to agricultural Egypt. One of the most vivid stories of the clash between nomads and farmers is the one about

Cain and Abel. Abel herds sheep; Cain is at first working the land. These brothers stood in each other's way; the nomad was killed. The transition between nomad and farmer is still fluid in those centuries. Cain wanders and becomes the forefather of shepherds, wandering musicians and blacksmiths. Thus to fratricide they ascribed in Israel the emergence of a semi-nomadic tribe, the Kenites. Out of these the father-in-law of Moses, Jethro, would come.

The transition to agriculture resulted in the cohabitation of larger groups. It allowed for the emergence of cities, since farmers produced more than needed for their own families. These new technologies did not merely result in an economic transition; value systems had to change as well. Such new circumstances will have resulted in stress; stress which was resolved in modified rituals. The place and responsibilities of each individual in the social structure had to be indicated and internalized. That is also one of the functions of the commandments of the Old Testament, including those which in general terms are still ours (such as 'the Ten Commandments') as well as those which we lay aside as rules from a time and world which is now gone.

For all those millennia religions seem not to have been oriented towards change or redemption, but towards the maintenance of personal, social and cosmic order. The priests and the powerful were on the same side. In the context of their religion people interpreted their lives, with its fortunes and misfortunes. The social order seemed obvious and unchangeable. In the context of the community one affirmed one's own position in life and accepted one's death.

Some centuries before the beginning of our era a new attitude emerged, and with it new types of religion. Karl Jaspers, who introduced this view of cultural history, spoke of the Axial Age. He thereby presented this period as a turning point in cultural history. This period, between 800 and 200 BCE, has been significant in different regions on our globe. In Greece there were great philosophers such as Socrates, Plato and Aristotle. In Israel prophets such as Isaiah, Jeremiah, Amos and Hosea were active. In Persia there was Zoroaster, in India Gautama (Buddha) and Mahavira, the founder of Jainism, and in China Confucius and Lao Tze (Taoism). The world religions arose alongside of the tribal religions.

It is risky to emphasize common aspects of developments in all these regions; differences in cultural traditions are significant. However, in various ways one of the fruits of the changes in these centuries was a greater sense of *individual* responsibility. The continuation of the tribe or community with its fixed positions and role expectations was no longer primary, but rather the focus was on the individual and what he or she could become. Besides, the social and cosmic order is no longer affirmed. Instead, our current earthly existence is felt lacking. In the religious myths our lives are confronted with something different, something better. In Hinduism this is redemption out of the cycles of earthly existence, in Buddhism it is Nirvana and Enlightenment. Among Jews the expectation of a Kingdom of God develops; in Christianity this longing returns also with a more individual focus as expectations about redemption and eternal life.

In consequence, whereas earlier religions affirmed one's place in the course of events, the world religions also nourished prophetic *protest*. The prophets in Israel were not fortune-tellers divining the future. Rather they were individuals who came forward to speak to the king and the people about their doings and dealings. Prophetic texts have something ominous; they announce judgment on those who do not live rightly. But they also speak of hope when the people lost confidence. The prophetic religiosity that has emerged in history out of the tribal religious traditions integrates criticism and longing. Faith is no longer mainly about powers that we do not understand or control. Faith becomes also the confrontation with situations in reality that we do not want to accept. To articulate this critical dimension, there is a dualistic element in religious images, a contrast between what is and what should be, whether articulated in the pair of earth and heaven, or as the city of men and the city of God, or as the present and the Kingdom, nature and grace, or in one of many other ways.

A few centuries later, someone asked Jesus what was the most important commandment. Jesus returned the question: 'What do you yourself think?' Upon which the one who asked answered: 'To love God with all your heart, and with all your soul, and with all your strength, and with all your mind; and your neighbour as yourself'. Then he asked Jesus whom he had to count as his neighbours. How far does this extend? Then Jesus told a story of 'one of us' who had been attacked while on the road. A priest passed by. One of us, but he did nothing. An assistant of the temple passed by. One of us, but he too did not help. A man from Samaria came by. Not one of us; the Samaritans were not our friends, but this stranger halted, he took care of the wounded man and brought him to an inn. When he had to leave, this Samaritan even left some money so that the innkeeper would continue caring for the man.

Jesus told stories. Stories about Jesus are told. Those stories have found their way into faith in miracles and have resulted in complicated theological constructions, for instance about the relationship between Jesus and God. In my opinion, more important than such speculative interpretations of Jesus are the parables, the Sermon on the Mount and the other stories. I believe that we primarily should seek to share the faith *of* Jesus, rather than faith *in* Jesus. In the attention given to those who were excluded, in the invitation to those who did not expect a future, as for instance the 'lost son', the prophetic protest and longing speaks to us. Boundaries are abandoned; the stranger takes care of the beaten.

INTERMEZZO: THE NATURE OF THEOLOGY

At this point, I want to digress from the grand tour 'from nothing until now' to offer some reflections on the nature of theology. In writing the way I have written above, I implicitly opt for a particular view of what theology might be in our time.

Let me begin with describing a position I reject, theology as the science of God. Biology is knowledge of the living (bios), psychology of the psyche, sociology is about social processes. Thus, 'theology' presents itself, at least linguistically, as knowledge of God (theos). A problematic issue is how we acquire such knowledge. On the basis of personal experiences? miracles? science? a holy book?

Personal experiences do not form, in my opinion, a good basis for knowledge of God. Human experiences do not reach that far. Extraordinary experiences, such as those of overwhelming silence, deep loneliness, wild ecstasy or deep communion with someone else, remain human experiences, shaped by our background, upbringing and situation. Experiences may be transformative, and we may start to see the world differently in consequence of what we have experienced. However, that does not yet make an intense personal experience the basis for science, not even a 'science of God'. What is rare is not thereby outside of our scientifically inspired view of reality. The integrity of reality (scenes 3 and 7) has been confirmed again and again. 'Miracles', unexpected events, are not the end of our knowledge but an occasion for further research. Miracles, extraordinary events, are in my opinion not a good basis for theology as a science.

It is, in my opinion, a very good thing for faith if we do not give miracles a place in our view of natural reality. Emphasis on miracles may give the impression that faith is about explaining events for which there is no scientific explanation. Such faith runs the risk of becoming a 'God of the gaps', withdrawing again and again on a smaller territory. It also offers a problematic conception of God: God leaves control mostly to the automatic pilot, but sometimes feels the need to change to manual control to correct mistakes in God's own design. Faith emphasizing miracles is also problematic in pastoral and moral perspective. If God does an occasional miracle, why not more often? Why not with this patient, this friend of mine, this suffering child? Why did God not push another sperm cell in the case of an Austrian couple at the end of the nineteenth century, giving them a daughter rather than their son Adolph? If God can intervene to deflect evil, why would we then have to take responsibility?

Rather than building upon miracles and personal experiences one might seek a firm basis in a book such as the Bible. But why not the Koran or another ancient text? Confidence can also be placed in persons such as martyrs, theologians of the early church, popes and bishops, teachers and mothers who have passed on the faith. Or gurus, masters and spiritual mediums. But why ascribe authority to this person rather than to that one? If I had been born in India, would I not have had different convictions? Even within a single tradition opinions diverge. The Biblical writings are no unity, as became clear when they became the subject of historical-critical investigation (see below, scene 9). Some stories were told in the palace or the temple, whereas others were told among farmers or shepherds. We too make out of this 'library' our own selection; some parts we consider to be important, while other texts are left in the background or read in a 'creative' way. We cannot trust blindly books or people. We always have to face the question: 'And why do you consider this wisdom?'

The exact sciences seem to offer more certainty. Once the mathematics teacher has proved the Pythagorean theorem (about the length of the hypotenuse of a rectangular triangle), the pupil seems to have no choice; whether understood or not, whether they like it or not, the teacher is right. Theology has from time to time looked for secure support from the sciences. Some hope that cosmology offers an argument or even a proof for the existence of God: there has been a beginning of the universe, any beginning needs a cause, hence there is a cause surpassing the universe. However, such a proof is not conclusive. As we have seen the concept of time is problematic (scene 1), and thus so is the whole notion of an absolute beginning and of anything preceding such a beginning. Such arguments also fail as they change domain, from explanations within reality to a statement about the ground of being. The success of science is paid for by a limitation of its ambitions. In my opinion the natural sciences may point us towards limit questions, but they do not get us across that boundary (scene 2).

Once upon a time there was a theology professor who taught on the attributes of God, including the unknowable ones. Knowledge of the unknowable has not been granted to me; human knowledge does not reach that far and deep. That is a good thing. The pretension to know exactly what God is like and wants from us easily generates intolerance. Awareness that God, the Ground of being, the absolutely good, is beyond our reach, may keep us from fanaticism.

Rather than understanding theology as the science of God, claiming knowledge, some have argued that we should concentrate on our limitations. When we speak of God as 'mystery' we admit that we do not have knowledge of God, while at the same time referring to God. That the sacred cannot be measured with any human measure, is pre-eminently a religious sensibility. To pretend to know God is the road to idolatry.

In the Bible the elusive, hidden character of God is considered at many places. Jacob wrestled with a stranger when crossing the Jabbok (Genesis 32). They struggle during the night; the stranger cannot be seen in daylight and his name is not revealed. The Name that Moses hears at the burning bush, sometimes translated as 'I am who I am' (Exodus 3: 14), is not a metaphysical description. Rather, it expresses an expectation; it is also open to the translation 'I will be who I will be'. At Mount Sinai there is a reference to 'a thick darkness where God was' (Exodus 20: 21). No images of God were accepted in Israel. A man takes a piece of wood from the forest. 'Half of it he burns in the fire; over half he eats flesh, he roasts meat and is satisfied; also he warms himself and says "Aha, I am warm, I have seen the fire!" And the rest of it he makes into a god, his idol; and falls down to it, and worships it; he prays to it and says "Deliver me, for thou art my god!"' (Isaiah 44: 16–17). Thus, Isaiah exposes the foolishness of falling down before a block of wood – and we could extend that to human images. Nor is final wisdom to be found among humans; only God 'understands the way to it, and he knows its place' (Job 28: 23); see also Proverbs 8 on wisdom's affinity to God. Job places his hand on his mouth and is silent (40: 4). Any human answer falls short; God is not according to human images. Job does not admit moral guilt but hubris that arose out of moral innocence.

In Jesus too God's presence is hidden and disputed. Is this the one we were expecting? 'Is not this the carpenter, the son of Mary and brother of James and Josef and Judas and Simon, and are not his sisters here with us?' (Mark 6: 3). He is unable even to come down from the cross. But then there is a Roman officer who says 'Truly this man was the Son of God!' (Mark 15: 39). Of the biblical God it can be said that as Lord he can be servant, in smallness great, in humiliation he shows his majesty.

These examples, which can be multiplied, show that there are many 'negative' moments in the Bible. They have to do with God's unknowability, mystery and holiness. Among the prophets there is another motive as well, outrage at social injustice: 'This cannot be God's intention; God is different'. The subsequent tradition does not live from a holy place where God is present, but from special moments of remembrance and expectation. The Sabbath recalls creation and anticipates its completion. In synagogue and church God's great deeds are called into memory with an eye on the future. For Jews and Christians the presence of God became a matter of recollection and hope, and thereby a matter of inner confidence, of faith. Life is oriented towards *The Elusive Presence* as the Bible scholar Samuel Terrien expressed it.

Later European critiques of too pretentious a religion could also appeal to the Greek philosophers. Xenophanes (d. 470 BCE) wrote that if they could, horses and oxen would think of the gods as horses and oxen. Our images are culturally shaped and anthropomorphic. Mythological stories about the gods are not adequate. The divine principle is different from all mortals. According to Plato's *Apology* Socrates was condemned to death since he did not acknowledge the gods of the city. Where others held to convictions, Socrates posed questions.

Plato adds another step. Critical questioning brings him to the idea that there must be a beginning, an *archè* from which everything springs forth. This theme is developed further in the neo-platonism of Plotinus. The One is beyond being. We can speak only of the One by denial, by negative predicates, as unbounded, timeless, infinite. Philo of Alexandria, a Jewish thinker from the beginning of our Common Era, identifies 'the One' with the biblical God.

Negative theology comes to a pinnacle in Christianity at the end of the fifth century with an author who is referred to as (pseudo) Dionysius the Areopagite. He wants to ascend from the image via the imageless to God. The road to God is not one of extrapolation but of denial, of abandoning our images and descriptions. With respect to the divine all negations are true, all affirmations are insufficient. The road aims via negation of all positions at a position beyond all negations. Dionysius assumed a hierarchical view of the world. Again and again there was a higher level to be reached by negating the lower one.

Just as in negative theology no answer is ever final, so too for the natural sciences. With every answer we can pose new questions (scene 2). In this way we may argue that there is an open place in our view of the world. We should handle that open place, those limit questions with care. If we draw images from our religious heritage to offer an explanation (God as 'creator') it may seem as if we claim to have knowledge 'beyond the knowable'. The Platonic philosophers could do that since they assumed a framework which to them was obvious. We no longer possess a generally accepted metaphysical framework of this kind; limit questions do not automatically lead us to a reasonable basis for faith.

If a 'science of God' is beyond our reach, theology can be seen as the study of religions as human phenomena. Such an understanding of theology can satisfy ordinary criteria of academic life. One can study how religious festivals organize social life around sowing and harvesting, birth, adulthood and death. One can analyse how Roman emperors strengthened their power by presenting themselves as gods to be worshipped; or pay attention to the way reconciliation within a tribe is reinforced by rituals. Anthropologists and sociologists have studied many different cultures around the world; the western cultures included. We too have our myths and rituals, both old and new.

As said in the introduction, when myths are considered as claims regarding that which once upon a time actually happened, they are ripe for the dust bin or the museum. Myths and masks become curiosities from times when 'they did not know better'. If they are seen as early stages of science and philosophy, they are outdated in the light of modern science. However, anthropologists, sociologists and students of literature have long noticed that a creation story is not merely about particular facts. These stories reflect human fears, passion and aggression, power and order. Myths have a normative role; they structure society and guide the individual. In this sense, myths are what the Bible calls *torah*, essential instruction. The anthropologist Clifford Geertz described a religion as

> a system of symbols which acts to establish powerful, pervasive, and long-lasting moods and motivations in men by formulating conceptions of a general order of existence and clothing these conceptions with such an aura of facticity that the moods and motivations seem uniquely realistic.

They are symbols and rituals motivating humans, and they achieve this by evoking certain ideas about the most basic order of existence. The worldview has to be perceived as rooted in 'the way things are', but the stories may well refer to this order indirectly, metaphorically. If the factual content of the stories is secondary to their guiding, comforting and life structuring function, we need not ask whether Noah's Ark was capable of holding all those animals and go search for remains. The story of the Great Flood is not important as a story about the distant past; it is important for us now as a story about the evil that we people do.

Theology as a science of God is beyond our grasp. Theology as religious studies is academically okay. However, it has a major disadvantage – one's own convictions can be left aside. One can study the opinions of a Christian theologian of the third century, an heretic of the twelfth century, a Buddhist leader, a Siberian shaman or a leader of a tribe of native Americans – and never speak about one's own convictions. Thus, one would bypass the questions that make theology interesting and valuable. Questions directed at oneself: How do you see life? What is of ultimate value for you? Adam, Eve, where are you? Or, less individualistic: What kind of community would we like to be? What kind of society? I see theologies as interpretations of existence with the help of particular religious heritages. In such an interpretation of existence, normative and factual elements are combined, just as they were mixed in creation stories and other myths.

When one articulates and justifies a particular interpretation of existence, issues of truth and of value are at stake. Debates about truth surpass the boundaries of religious studies but still are academically respectable. In considering the value of a particular tradition, theology goes beyond the regular territory of academia, though it does so in the good company of normative ethics, social philosophy and aesthetics.

Typical of theologies, as systematic positions, seems to be that they offer a particular view of the way the world is *and* a view of the way the world should be, thus of the True and the Good, of the real and the ideal. Each theology is a particular view of the relationship between a cosmology (in the metaphysical sense as a view of the way the world is) and an axiology, that is, a view of the values that should be realized. About a century ago William James wrote in *The Varieties of Religious Experience* on the difference 'whether one accepts the universe in the drab discolored way of stoic resignation to necessity, or with the passionate happiness of Christian saints'. 'At bottom the whole concern of both morality and religion is with the manner of our acceptance of the universe. Do we accept it only in part and grudgingly, or heartily and altogether? Shall our protests against certain things in it be radical and unforgiving, or shall we think that, even with evil, there are ways of living that must lead to good?'

Thus, as a heuristic formulation that may help to clarify and explore a complex area of discussion I suggest the 'formula':

$$\text{a theology} = \text{a cosmology} + \text{an axiology}$$

(with the + sign not being a mere addition, but hiding the crucial issue of how the two are brought together).

Theologies can be quite different in the way they relate cosmological and axiological aspects. One can have a scientistic 'theology' when on the basis of explanatory insights, e.g. about the evolution of human behaviour, one makes statements on the behaviour we ought to display or the values that we should adhere to. Such a 'theology' is fully dominated by the cosmological pole. To take a different example, when Fritjof Capra wrote in his book *The Turning Point* that inflation, unemployment and pollution 'are all different facets of one and the same crisis, and that this crisis is essentially a crisis of perception' which will be overcome in an 'ecological perspective', he implicitly offered a cosmology and axiology in one, namely the view that there are no genuine conflicts of interests in the world, if we take the proper perspective. There is no tragic choice between two evils, no falling short; essentially, it is all a crisis of perception, a matter of the way we see the world.

Within the Christian tradition, there are – upon my definition – various theologies. When the emphasis is on God's saving activity, the tension between the way the world is and the way it will be, is prominent, whereas in creation-oriented views (whether ecologically inspired or as natural theologies) cosmology and axiology stand less in contrast. The prophet might emphasize the tension, whereas the mystic might stress the way we belong to reality.

The attempt to combine 'is' and 'ought' statements is what makes theology so problematical, so difficult and so valuable. This difficulty again and again finds expression in the problem of evil, which typically concerns the relationship or tension between the two main components. Such an understanding of theology as 'cosmology-and-axiology' gives a particular role to theology, while respecting the autonomy of science and also, less openly acknowledged, of moral discourse. It is in those domains that secular rationality has its primary rights.

Upon this view, one can distinguish between science and an interpretation of science, which is a cosmology, metaphysics or philosophy of nature. A cosmology, in this sense, is a view of what the world (with its substances and relations, matter, forces and causality) might be like, given what we know. Any such metaphysics is an interpretation of scientific knowledge, constrained but underdetermined by the sciences.

As far as religion is concerned, the definition places the emphasis on existential issues which become prominent when our reality is not in agreement with what we think ought to be, rather than on supernatural or magical elements which upset our understanding of the cosmology without taking into account the relationship with the axiological. Religion can thus be thought about critically, not as being about that which upsets the cosmological order, but rather about the way convictions regarding values and facts are related – in harmony or in tension – even though the particular existential view on 'what is' and 'what ought to be' may well be beyond rational defence.

Critical thought

Look,
> *measure*
> *and count,*
> *challenge knowledge*
> *and authority!*
Enlightenment
> *way out of immaturity.*

The rise of the natural sciences is, with hindsight, one of the greatest transitions in human history, perhaps comparable only to the emergence of agriculture (see scene 8). It is a pinnacle of self-critical thinking. What was involved in this revolution? New instruments such as the telescope and the microscope opened new worlds. Mathematics was applied to describe reality. Experiments were used to test ideas. Such experiments often dealt with situations that were unrealistically simple: balls rolling down inclined planes, pendulums swinging regularly, etc. Theories developed and tested in those simplified realities turned out to be applicable well beyond their original context. These theories have become more and more adequate over time, once scientists incorporate in their models more aspects of the processes concerned. In recent years the study of complex and chaotic systems has become a booming business. These systems are of such a complexity that one cannot predict the future of the system in full detail, even though the actual development can be clearly understood *post factum*. The weather is a familiar example; all mechanisms involved are understood, but still we cannot predict reliably what the weather will be three weeks from now – and we know why we are unable to make such predictions.

Science has not only enlarged our view of the world, giving us access to new worlds. Science also resulted in the abandonment of ideas, also of ideas that accurately described ordinary experience. When we throw a ball it will come to a halt, unless we make an effort to keep it moving. The physics of Aristotle reflected this experience well, but in high school the science teacher tells of Newton's First Law: an object maintains its movement unless an effort is made to slow it down. Not only common sense ideas about movement are modified, but also ideas about substance. A solid, massive object has no empty space inside – but according to atomic physics a solid object is mostly empty space between atomic nuclei and electrons. New domains of reality have been explored, while ideas about already familiar aspects of reality have been abandoned and modified. Not only have we gone further in space and further back in time, but ideas about space and time themselves have changed (see scenes 1 and 3). Learning physics is not merely a training in mathematics and theories, as if it is all about information about reality. It is also a training in flexibility, in being open to objections, in being prepared to forgo former ideas if they do not match reality.

The most important book of the nineteenth century is Charles Darwin's *The Origin of Species by Means of Natural Selection* (1859). Since then, species are seen as the fruit of a long 'natural history'. Awareness of historical dimensions is one of the great achievements of European culture in the last few centuries. This not only showed in ideas about nature in geology, biology and, beginning in the twentieth century, cosmology, but also in ideas about culture.

The Bible too became an object of scientific research. Humans wrote those texts. Who? When did that take place? Why did they say it this way and not differently? What did they borrow from neighbouring cultures? Is the text a unity or more like a mosaic with pieces of different kinds? What is legend and what reliable? The Christian tradition was the first one that had to face such a historical, critical self-examination. What do we claim to offer? On what basis?

Critical thinking was not only applied to scientific and historical enquiry, but also manifested itself in a different kind of society. The authority of kings, nobility and clerics was challenged. The circle of respected persons expanded. Citizens acquired political rights, resulting in universal suffrage. Women became included as well. Slavery was abandoned. Changing political attitudes manifested themselves in the American Revolution, the French Revolution with its slogan of liberty, equality and brotherhood (1789), and, one and a half centuries later in the Universal Declaration of Human Rights (1948). Such ideals have never been fully realized. The twentieth century has seen horrendous atrocities. Still, such public statements and, for instance, the public support for Amnesty International exemplify a social and political development of major importance. Resistance against cruelty towards animals signals a further widening of the circle in this respect.

At the end of the eighteenth century, the philosopher Immanuel Kant labelled the Enlightenment as an exodus out of a self-inflicted immaturity. That it was self-inflicted I am not so sure of; immaturity was an unavoidable part of our heritage, but these centuries have been an exodus out of immaturity. People have never before been as aware of the possibility to test knowledge claims and to call authority into question, while relying on knowledge which has withstood the test of substantial questioning, proving itself to be robust. Together these elements have generated a mixture of 'modernity' that has spread from Europe across the globe.

I consider this as a great gift. We have discovered something valuable. Sometimes we have been too optimistic about 'reason' and 'civilization'. Sometimes, our biases have been grossly neglected. Injustice has been done in the name of 'civilization' and 'reason' – but even more injustices and cruelties have arisen due to denial of the ideals of equal rights and critical testing. We should not out of a sense of guilt close our eyes to the important changes in these centuries. The rise of the natural sciences, of historical consciousness, of the political ideals of freedom and equality, and of the social role of democratic societies are not merely products of a particular culture, exchangeable for insights and ideals from any other culture or epoch. They are morally inspired moments in the development of a critical attitude with respect to moral claims and purported knowledge, in the development of opposition to totalitarian regimes and power based on violence and arbitrary authority. Scientific insights and attitudes contributed to 'higher' forms of life. 'Higher' not in a biological sense, but spiritual, as growth in moral sensibility and critical thinking.

Openness to the self-correcting, self-critical effects of science and to historical insight with its support for some relativism has shaped liberal forms of religion, and these developments have triggered responses. Rather than responding with openness, being prepared to learn and change, some have withdrawn from modern culture into their own citadel of certainties. Fundamentalism is not so much the continuation of an old tradition as a response to these new developments, digging the heels into the sand, sometimes even resorting to violence.

Christian self-criticism has led some to appreciate wisdom from other cultures. Meditation techniques such as yoga from Asia have spread in Europe and America. There is much to be said for the appropriation of insights from others, at least as long as such steps are not accompanied by naive claims that, for instance, transcendental meditation would make social problems disappear easily, passing by realistic issues of social structures of domination. There is alas also too much credulity, apparently forgetting the moral and intellectual critical attitude that has risen. As exemplified by their longing for the alleged wisdom of angels, trees and lost continents, many seem to be searching again and again for the putative safety of an earlier, more magical and naive view of life. In my opinion, we ought rather to accept the challenge of intellectual maturity, to live with counter-intuitive insights and critical testing, the insecurity of not having final answers, and the never finished dialogue among all participants in our societies.

INTERMEZZO: THE NATURE OF KNOWLEDGE

At this point I want to digress, again, from the grand tour 'from nothing until now'. Both for the appeal made to the sciences in this book and for reflections on faith it is useful to explore the nature of science a bit further.

There are a variety of disciplines within the natural sciences. Physics concentrates on the unity in underlying laws and processes, whereas biology faces the variety of realizations of those laws. Chemistry is typically a lab science, whereas geology is primarily a field science. When one is interested in causal explanations, the focus often will be on physics. When the prime interest is in human experience, there will be a greater interest in relations between psychology, the neurosciences and biology and chemistry, that is, in issues of reductionism (see scene 8 and p. 73 below). When we focus on human actions and responsibility, we might pay attention primarily to sciences that transform reality, such as chemistry and engineering, rather than to more descriptive sciences such as geology.

There are not only different disciplines. Within each discipline there are theories of different standing. Some have withstood tests under a wide range of conditions. A good example might be the ideas expressed in chemistry in the periodic table of the elements. The scheme is, as any scientific theory, in principle provisional. However, there is no serious challenge for this description of matter, at least at ordinary temperatures and pressures. It is accepted in a wide variety of cultures. Ideas about atoms and their properties are used daily in pharmaceutical and industrial contexts. The scheme is intelligible in relation to the physics of nuclei and electrons. Both in theory and in practice, the insight that matter is constituted of atoms of various kinds is very well established. As other examples of consolidated knowledge, one might think of neo-Darwinian evolutionary theory and the idea that the Earth is more or less spherical.

Apart from such consolidated knowledge there are ideas that are corroborated only to a certain extent. One might perhaps compare the situation within any discipline to a layered cup.

At the bottom, there is consolidated science. The fluid represents current research; there is some consolidation, but it is not fully consolidated yet. Bubbles in the air correspond to more speculative ideas: they may evaporate without leaving a trace, but can also condense and become part of more consolidated knowledge.

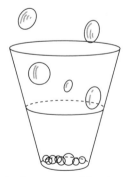

Figure 2 The layered cup of science, consolidated and speculative.

Contemporary natural science is stable in the sense that many branches of science build upon knowledge acquired in the last few centuries. Whereas there was a time when the existence of atoms was seriously disputed, it now seems extremely unlikely that physicists and chemists ever will abandon belief in atoms and in the periodic table arranging the various elements. It seems equally unlikely that biologists will abandon evolution, both as a view of the natural history of organisms, and as a theory explaining this natural history in terms of transmission of properties (in genes) and of differences in survival and reproduction between various variants. However, science is also provisional. This provisional character is not merely a consequence of extending our knowledge into new domains. We may also acquire a deeper understanding of domains already known, and thereby modify our views. For instance, our understanding of the particles that make up atoms (protons, neutrons) has changed; they now are taken to consist of quarks and gluons. If one probes further 'inside' the atom, one comes into a domain where the physics is very speculative, and certainly not as stable as our belief in atoms.

When it comes to speculative issues, for instance in cosmological theories regarding the very early universe, it is hard to distinguish between the marginal and the speculative. However, there are also examples of marginal science that run counter to consolidated science. Religious believers, and especially New Age authors, often seem to prefer marginal science, as if that would be more open to spiritual insights than mainstream science. However, inventing or picking one's own science does not contribute at all to the reflection on religion and human concerns in relation to the really existing sciences. It is dishonest to one's audience. If a spiritual thinker has a bright idea on how to change the science, that idea might be brought forward in front of the proper audience, the scientific community. If the professionals consider the modification to be a serious option, then it becomes an idea worth pursuing in the religious community as well, but not the other way round.

A major characteristic of the sciences is their wide scope; their domain seems to be without obvious boundaries. Terrestrial physics turned out to be applicable to heavenly phenomena as well, and chemistry can be applied to processes in living beings. The domain of the sciences extends from the smallest objects to the universe at large, from extremely brief phenomena to the stability of rocks, and from heavy objects to massless light.

Correlated with the extension of science is the inner coherence of our scientific knowledge. The coherence between different sciences has proved to be a heuristically fruitful guide in the development of the sciences, and, if temporarily strongly violated, has at least re-established itself as a result of later scientific developments. Coherence, the unity of the sciences, has on the basis of our experiences become a criterion which makes us reject, or at least consider with the utmost suspicion, purported knowledge which stands in splendid isolation, even if it would not conflict with the rest of our knowledge.

Science is taken by me in a *realist* way in the sense that it is assumed to study a reality that is to a large extent independent of us. Even the study of human consciousness by physiologists and psychologists is in many cases the study of other persons, and if it is self-reflection there still is the assumption that the reflection concerns one's own inner feelings and thoughts – a reality on which one reflects.

However, such a realism does not carry us very far in debates on *scientific realism*, which are, in my view, not debates about the existence of 'reality out there' but debates about the quality of our knowledge. Do our terms refer to entities out there? Can we say that these entities exist? Do our theories express relations between entities out there? Or, less generally, which theories, or which elements in our theories, can we take seriously as 'depicting' the way reality is? Unqualified realism seems too strong, and thus too vulnerable to criticisms. Scientific explanations and concepts are provisional human constructs organizing the natural world; they are not independent of human intellectual capacities, social interactions, and contingencies of history, even though one can still speak meaningfully of *The Advancement of Science*, as the philosopher Philip Kitcher titled a book.

In science there is more risk involved than in formal demonstrations (as in mathematics) since the scientific theories are not in a strict sense implied by the data. The development of scientific theories is also more risky than generalization, since theories may postulate entities and concepts of a kind not found in the data; theories are more than generalizations of facts. Debates about scientific realism can also be interpreted as debates about the way we should consider the theories of science given the 'risk' involved in the process by which we come to these theories: is the process to be understood as a form of inference on which we can rely (and to what extent and for what purposes)?

Scientific theories offer us *scientific images* of the world, that is, images that differ from our *manifest images*. This is especially relevant when we consider religion, since religion is in general intimately related to manifest images. This has to do with the importance of tradition for religion, and hence that of symbols and myths from earlier times. It has also a 'public relations' side, since most religions reach out to a wide audience that understands and relates to manifest images more easily.

INTERMEZZO: OUR KNOWLEDGE OF NATURE

The combination of diversity and coherence in the sciences seems to reflect properties of reality. There is a variety of different 'levels of complexity', while there are also relations between those levels – relations that suggest integration of one kind or another, an integration often labelled 'reductionism'.

One can use the label 'naturalism' for worldviews that follow the natural sciences as their major guide for understanding the world in which we live and of which we are a part.

With respect to our ideas about 'what there is' (ontology), naturalism is the view that assumes that all objects around us, including ourselves, consist of the stuff described by chemists in the periodic table of the elements. This stuff is further understood by physicists to consist of elementary particles and forces, and beyond that is assumed to consist of quantum fields, superstrings, or whatever. As the 'whatever' indicates, our knowledge has not reached rock bottom yet. Hence, naturalism cannot be articulated on the basis of a fundamental ontology, a complete inventory of the world. Nor does naturalism imply that all phenomena can be described in terms of physics and chemistry, as we will see when we come to discuss reductionism. A naturalist can hold that there are genuinely new objects with new properties, even though they have arisen out of other objects.

With respect to history, naturalism understands living beings – again, including ourselves – as the current stage in a bundle of Darwinian evolutionary histories on our planet, which itself is seen as a transient phenomenon in a universe that has been expanding for some fifteen billion years. These insights do not commit one to a particular view on processes 'within the first fraction of the first second'; it may be that 'the first second' is not an adequate reference at all. With respect to history too, fundamental issues about the beginning of our universe are not settled. There is an irresolvable open end to our understanding – an openness which allows one to believe in a Beyond which brings forth this world (theism), a divinity which would be intrinsic to nature (pantheism), or to present oneself as an agnostic (we will never know). A naturalistic view of reality allows for more than one religious interpretation.

Naturalism considers social and mental life as two of the fruits of the long evolutionary process. We are not exceptions to reality but rather remarkable manifestations of reality. One can think of science and other intellectual enterprises as building upon human capacities for dealing with their environment, improved piecemeal over the course of many generations. Science is a social phenomenon which is cognitively reliable, and increasingly so. However, when we come to social and mental life, we also have to acknowledge the richness of human experience – a richness which science seems unable to catch explicitly in its theories.

Wildness of experience

As the novelist John Fowles expressed it in *The Tree*:

> Ordinary experience, from waking second to second, is . . . hopelessly beyond science's powers to analyse. It is quintessentially 'wild', in the sense my father disliked so much: unphilosophical, uncontrollable, incalculable. In fact it corresponds very closely – despite our endless efforts to 'garden', to invent disciplining social and intellectual systems – with wild nature. Almost all the richness of our personal existence derives from this synthetic and eternally present 'confused' consciousness of both internal and external reality, and not least because we know it is beyond the analytical, or destructive, capacity of science.

Understanding human experiences and religions in the context of our scientific image of the world should not be achieved by pruning lightly, that is, by denying complex, 'wild' experiences for the sake of simplicity.

Sometimes, our inability to analyse our experiences is due to the models of reality we use. For example, metaphors borrowed from technology are used to make sense of our experiences; 'letting off steam' and 'being under pressure' are metaphors which depend on nineteenth-century technology; 'recharging batteries' and 'tuning in' reflects the earlier electromechanical technology, and the personal computer era has generated a whole new set of metaphors. This use of metaphors derived from technology is fine as long as their metaphorical character is kept in mind. However, if the analogy between humans and technical artefacts, from clocks to computers, is made too tight, it becomes ridiculous; 'wild nature', including human nature, is richer than such technological metaphors can express.

As I see it, the wildness of experiences is related to various limitations that manifest themselves almost everywhere in nature. For example, as humans we are unable to monitor our inner states. Furthermore, the causal webs of responding to the environment are the product of such a long, convoluted evolutionary history and embryological development as to be beyond detailed analysis. We are also limited with respect to detailed explanations of particular events. Chaos theory has made clear what could have been obvious to students of historical evidence: we never have sufficient knowledge of all details as to provide a full account of the course of events. Besides, a full account would be so cumbersome as to be unmanageable and inaccessible to us.

There is also a limitation of a more conceptual kind: sciences describing higher, more complex levels of reality need concepts that are not adequately expressible in the concepts of physics. They cut the pie of reality in different ways into intelligible units and processes, and the wider context may have to be taken into account in different ways (especially when it comes to issues such as the meaning of language). This shows up especially clearly in the relationship between biology on the one hand and physics and chemistry on the other. In physics and chemistry phenomena are primarily classified in terms of what they do and of their micro-structure, whereas in biology phenomena are primarily classified in terms of their purpose and function. In biology there is a greater variety of types of explanations, since one may explain in functional terms what happens, in causal terms how it happens, and in evolutionary terms why the organism is structured so that this behaviour can happen.

Science now is able to face more than the 'garden' where reality is pruned as to make it manageable to science; 'wild' reality comes in sight again. From the richness of our manifest images we have first restricted ourselves to the study of gross simplifications, and then reconstructed from insights about these simplifications an understanding of more complex phenomena. We have gone through many cycles of simplification and building up again towards an understanding of complex phenomena. As a consequence of the detour through the study of simpler systems, science now more fully understands 'wild' reality in its variety and at the same time its own limitations in explanatory and predictive power.

The conviction that science is unable to account for 'wild' nature is to some extent true: it is not able to predict events in full detail. However, science has over time become better and better at understanding complex phenomena. Unlike Fowles's suggestion, such an understanding need not be destructive. To be fair to science, we should not dismiss science on the basis of straw men, that is, models, simple theories and initial approximations. Nor, however, should a scientist dismiss lightly phenomena on the basis of too simplistic models of reality.

At some places the distance between our manifest and scientific images may be minimal; at other places it may be more significant. If we find ourselves with two images, which one is more important? That depends on the purpose. It may well be that the 'wild' richness of experiences is more important when we deal with one another as humans, when we long for consolation, for a sense of beauty, et cetera. The scientific image, however, has gone through a critical process of articulation with precision and testing, and is therefore more adequate when we are after 'intellectual adequacy' since that is what it has been selected for.

In and through the sciences we have come up with all kinds of scientific images that differ significantly from the way we experience the world, our manifest images. This can be explained further when we consider two different ways of using the word 'experience'. 'I experienced a tree' can be said in two ways. It can be a description about how something seems to me, without regard to the accuracy of that seeming. I may say 'I experienced a tree, but then I realized I was mistaken.' Experience is also used as an achievement word; 'I experienced a tree' if it not only appeared to me that there was a tree, but there was a real tree which I saw or felt. We cannot and should not seek to explain away experiences as people have them – 'experience' in the first sense indicated above. However, it is a fair game of science to offer explanations that differ from the person's initial explanation. No one is infallible with respect to the underlying processes, even if one is honest in reporting about what one believes to have seen. We know all too well how we can be fooled by illusions, triggered by clues that we do not take into account consciously (as is so well exploited in advertising). We can easily fool ourselves, intentionally or unintentionally, by creating explanations that seem to make our actions seem rational and justified.

Reduction is not elimination, but rather affirmation

Some are worried by reductionist explanations since they fear that successful reduction eliminates the phenomena considered. However, this is mistaken. Discerning the physiological basis for a trait affirms its reality. Genes are not less real for being understood as strands of DNA, and pain is not less real if physiologically understood. Rather the opposite: if the doctor can locate the bodily process underlying my pain, my friends will take my complaints with more seriousness. Any scientific description of a table – even when understood as mostly empty space with a few electrons and nuclei – will have to incorporate the fact that I cannot put my hand through the table, unless with considerable force and with major consequences for the table and for my hand. We may have to give up some philosophical notions attached to substance, but we do not eliminate common-sense solidity.

Tables and trees, humans and bees: we all consist of atoms: hydrogen, carbon, oxygen and the like. If one takes anything apart, one will not find additional substances. This has brought some to a negative statement of human worth. If we were to buy in the cheapest way the ingredients necessary for a human being, we would not need to spend much: we need water, some rusty nails (for the iron in our blood), some matches for the phosphorus, some charcoal for the carbon, etc. A human does not add up to much. That may seem to be a message from the sciences.

However, if one continues this assessment of the economic worth of humans, there is something else – the costs of labour to put it all together in the right way. Labour has been invested in us, by our parents, partners, friends, and teachers and by ourselves, from embryological development to reading dull books. There also has been labour invested in the construction of humans during our whole past cultural and evolutionary history. That too is part of the 'value' of a human being – and that drives up the price enormously. One could reconstitute out of the constituent parts a simple chemical substance quite easily (e.g. water out of hydrogen and oxygen), but to reconstitute a human from matter is way beyond what is, or will become feasible.

So what is this position I am trying to present? On the one hand, I am pleading for reductionism: we are nothing but matter. As far as the entities involved, reductionism seems true. Everything is composed of substance as studied by physics. What this substance is, is known in many ways – atoms and molecules, photons, quarks etc.; but deep down we do not have the ultimate foundation – as we develop physics from our range of experiences and delve deeper and deeper. This unfinished quest within physics brings us back to the issue of limit questions. Here, however, we do not focus on those limit questions but on the relation between 'higher levels' of reality and descriptions given by physics. In that context, I also object to certain forms of reductionism.

Let us consider a simple example: paying someone some money. Would that be an activity that we could describe in terms of physics? Every time you pay someone, there is a change in the physical world – coin or paper money changes place, bytes in the computer of the bank are set differently, etc. However, it would be very odd to describe the monetary transaction in terms of the physical change – as it is not just some atoms of copper, some pieces of paper, or some magnetic states that have changed. Nor would all transfers of paper or metal count as paying. The categories that are fruitful in understanding our world are different for economy than they are for physics. When it comes to money, the environment also plays an important role – the bytes are money only when the employees of the bank are willing to interpret the state of the computer thus.

There is an even stronger form of non-reductionism. In many cases the original entities do not exist anymore. When two atoms of hydrogen form one hydrogen molecule, there is a genuine new entity with new properties. It is not a bag with two balls in it. Rarely will one find someone who argues that current entities are not real as they came forth out of past ones. Why would one then deny the reality of higher level entities if they have emerged out of more elementary systems?

This, in a nutshell, is a common understanding of reality, inspired by the sciences. Everything is 'nothing but the stuff studied by physics', atoms and the like. But more complex entities, including us as human beings, are not adequately described by physics; we need concepts and explanations of many other kinds to do justice to the rich possibilities of nature. In the reflections on reductionism, we have combined two moves. There is a good case to be made against certain forms of reductionism. Higher levels are real, and they do need their own concepts in order to be described adequately. Pain does not become less real or painful when its physiological basis is unravelled. At the same time, some forms of reductionism seem to hold true; more complex entities are made out of more simple ones.

There are underlying processes. So what! Such a form of reduction is not elimination; rather, it is integration of these phenomena into our picture of the world. Such a reductionism might even be renamed as a form of holism!

Stories and arguments

This understanding of reality has consequences for the place science has in our world. The analytical, empirical and rational approach is enormously powerful. When calculations, experiments and arguments are adequate to a task, we would be ducking our responsibilities if we did not use them. However, many tasks are not amenable in the same way to analysis, experiment and argument, for instance the task we undertake in this book, thinking about our world. Academic philosophy needs to be argumentative and analytical. However, as humans we also tell stories. In this way we create worlds that – though our creations – are real for us, shape our identity and our way of life. The management of companies has over the last decade become more sensitive to mission statements, self-images and stories; our spiritual life has always lived from stories and images. Popular science literature too functions as myth; they locate us in a greater framework, often with existential connotations (as meaningless, amazing, beautiful, or whatever).

Modern humans live with myths, but also with critical thought. We are developing more and more refined ways of testing and observing. The scientific view of the world is not only knowledge of nature, but also a new view of the nature of knowledge. Self-criticism and testing are essential characteristics of science. They also reveal an attitude, a way of life. We use our best available theories, but when we have to abandon them, we ought to do so – the attitude is more important than any particular theory. As the philosopher of science Bas Van Fraassen says, in a criticism of those who are not willing to give up their beloved theories:

What is the alternative to reifying the content of science? The alternative is to accept the challenge of intellectual maturity: to let your faith be not a dogma but a search, not an answer but a question and a quest, and to immerse yourself in a new world-picture without allowing yourself to be swallowed up.

This is also how I would like to relate to the stories that can be found in our religious heritages and the theologies we construct. We appropriate them, we live with them, but we also question them, for their content and their consequences – and if necessary, we will abandon them. Using our critical faculties in a sensible way is a sign of intellectual and spiritual maturity. If one forgets that myths are human stories, we run the risk of dangerous dogmatism. When myths are taken as literal depictions of 'what happened', what the myths convey is lost. However, myths have a poetic power, the power to evoke emotions and attitudes, the power to trigger us into action. We ought not to inhabit only the world of the myths; we have to take our responsibility by analysing them, also to see what a myth evokes, for good or for evil.

Responsibility

In us
  our heritage,
  matter,
  information,
  and a box
  full of stories.
Between
  hope and fear
  our neighbours
  life
  here on Earth,
between
  hope and fear
  the great project
  of thought
  and compassion
on a road
  of freedom.

Taking stock

We carry with us, or rather, in our bodies, our language and culture, our heritage. Our heritage is *material*. The stuff out of which we are made is dust from stars (see scene 4). We inherit also *biological information*, useful recipes for making a human, recipes which have emerged in the course of a long history. Nature does not need a recipe to make salt out of sodium and chloride, but to create haemoglobin, the red oxygen-binding chemical in our blood, the body needs a recipe, instructions which are available in our genes, our DNA. Salt would form without any history; substances such as chlorophyll (in green plants) and haemoglobin are products of a history in which our heritage has been tested and expanded (see scenes 5 and 6). Our bodies, our brains with their potential, our responses: everything is a product of history, materialized as biological recipes. Again and again we have to do with our biological heritage. That is not a burden, but the basis of our existence. Thanks to this biological heritage we may feel, think and act.

Our heritage is also *cultural*. Human languages embody knowledge about the world. Different legal and political systems and etiquette show how people may live together. Religious traditions with their rituals and stories are part of our cultural heritage too. We inherited the critical traditions, the social critique of the prophets (see scene 8) and the intellectual and political critiques of modernity (see scene 9).

Our bodies and our cultures present well winnowed wisdom, tested in many generations. However, that does not imply that everything that has been wisdom in the past still is. An unrestricted 'Be fruitful and multiply' is no longer wisdom when six billion humans are filling and subduing the Earth. Wisdom is bound to circumstances, and these can change. Wisdom is also related to a goal; the wisdom physics offers is quite insignificant when facing the death of a friend.

Progress?

In these scenes we considered a long development. New possibilities emerged: heavy elements, life with purposiveness, humans with consciousness, science with explicitly articulated knowledge. Has this made the world a better place? Is this a history of progress?

In the twentieth century humans have massacred humans on an unprecedented scale. In itself, killing of others of one's own kind is nothing new. It is part of our history of the last millions of years. Similar behaviour has been observed among chimps. However, even if the frequency of killings has not increased, their efficiency sadly has. A relatively recent step has been the development of nuclear weapons that can destroy whole cities.

We humans are not only a threat to our fellow humans, but also to other species. This too has been going on for ages. When humans entered a new territory they first hunted the easiest prey. For the dodo on Mauritius the beginning of the end came when Dutch ships dropped their sails on its shores in 1507. Most of the big mammals of America became extinct some eleven thousand years ago, around the time ancestors of the native Americans crossed the Bering Strait. At Hawaii various birds disappeared when Polynesians discovered the island, 1500 years ago. Flightless birds were eaten to extinction by the Maoris of New Zealand. Species other than *homo sapiens* have shown similar behaviour. European cats and foxes imported to Australia have eaten the larger part of the small marsupials. Their decline is no threat to the predators themselves, since they change prey easily. Humans too are very flexible.

Some animals have finished it for themselves. Reindeer flourished on St Matthew Island in the Bering Sea: 1,350 reindeer in 1957, 6,000 in 1963. They ate lichen faster than it could recover. After the harsh winter of 1963–1964 there were left forty-one females and one sterile male. Early in the twentieth century rabbits were introduced on Lisianski, an island west of Hawaii. Within ten years they had eaten almost all plants on the island, thus undermining the conditions for their own existence. On the island Earth we may follow a similar course. We have no natural enemies that constrain the population size. Death toll due to contagious diseases has gone down enormously. We easily change prey, and modern technology has created the possibility of accelerated growth. We too can be caught by the ecological limitations of our own 'island', just as the reindeer of St Matthew and the rabbits of Lisianski.

An ecological crisis will not hurt all in the same way. Hence, ecological problems may generate conflicts about water, oil, heat and food. Let me give one example. Life in Europe is dependent upon the warm Gulf Stream that crosses the Atlantic from the Caribbean to north-west Europe. If, due to the greenhouse effect, there is more rain in the northern Atlantic Ocean this warm Gulf Stream might fall away. In consequence the climate in Europe would become similar to that of Canada; Newfoundland is south of the Netherlands. Canada houses and feeds less than thirty million inhabitants; Europe more than five-hundred million on a similar area. Would hundreds of millions set off to warmer regions? A change like this could happen fairly abruptly, in the course of a few years. It would have dramatic consequences for relations between countries. Whether the falling out of the Gulf Stream and subsequent lower temperatures in Europe is the right scenario, is not clear yet. Perhaps some other consequences of the human induced greenhouse effect may be more important. Whatever the particular events, changes in climate and ecology might create geopolitical tensions of an unprecedented scale.

Science and technology have expanded our capacity to modify our environment so that it better serves our needs. We can now intentionally modify all three aspects of our heritage described above. Setting up nuclear power plants, not to speak of nuclear weapons, reflects our ability to transform matter; chemistry and material sciences can create stuff with an incredible range of properties. Biotechnology is the ability to modify intentionally the informational heritage as coded in the genes, in humans and in plants, yeasts and animals that we eat. Our cultural heritage is changing due to the ability to store information in print and electronically, and even more to the ability to spread information across the globe. In a sense, there is progress in power, and thus in freedom, but it is progress with a prize; the risks are enormous as are the surprises due to unanticipated consequences.

Consequences are anticipated in utopian and dystopian literature. Frances Bacon's *Nova Atlantis*, from 1627, is the archetype of a utopia inspired by technology and science. Thomas More's *Utopia* (1516) is a vision of a better world, based on a well-designed social organization. Bacon's technological optimism contrasts with the pessimistic view of Aldous Huxley in his *Brave New World* (1932). George Orwell's *Animal Farm* (1945) can be seen as a counterpoint to the social utopia of a Thomas More. Social utopias, in the twentieth century represented by authoritarian regimes such as communism, seek to establish happiness by controlling human behaviour. Again and again they had to limit human freedom. A technological utopia seeks to control our environment.

Large segments of our culture have acquired features of a realized technical utopia. Quite a few technological developments predicted in Bacon's *Nova Atlantis* and Aldous Huxley's *Brave New World* have been realized, without however making our society into the technocratic one they envisaged. Our technology has not been anti-moral, but to some extent it has become an embodiment of our morality – with speed limits enforced by sleeping policemen and automatic cameras, etc. The great advantage of technological over social utopianism has been that it leaves one free to think – though it limits one's practical options – and it leaves us free to use the available means in a creative, unanticipated way. In many cases it is often morally more appropriate to develop technical means to implement certain behaviour than to seek to influence the mentality of the humans involved. We may call for more restraint in the use of energy, but more energy efficient heating systems and cars may make it actually possible to move in the desirable direction. We invest our technology with morality – and that may be appreciated.

Can we bear responsibility? What kind of beings are we?

If we are the product of evolution, can we take positive initiatives, make the right choices? Or are our choices fixed since days of old, and is freedom nothing but an illusion? Libraries could be filled with books on 'free will'. Here I want to indicate briefly why I hold that a meaningful notion of freedom might perhaps be integrated with a scientific view of the reality of which we humans are a part.

Freedom requires determinism, since responsibility assumes that our actions are related to their consequences. Otherwise one could not develop plans, anticipating the consequences of one's acts. Meaningful freedom is not the opposite of determination but is some form of self-determination. One might speak of freedom when my considerations, my principles, my character partly determine what happens. When others determine my acts, I bear no responsibility. When the juice I drink at breakfast determines my actions, freedom is impaired; we do not consider such drinks to be the relevant kind of determining factors. However, when my ideals determine my behaviour, freedom is not impaired but affirmed. Political freedom can be described by striking out external factors: freedom is real when one's behaviour is not determined by the state, nor by the church, nor by my neighbours, nor by my relatives, and so on. Personal freedom cannot be defined in such a way, as if freedom would consist in not being determined by one's character, nor by one's principles, one's life-plan, one's ideals.

Principles and ideals do not float in from nowhere; they too are products of nurture and nature. Hence, would one not be free since the past determines who you are and how you choose? This objection to freedom in the context of a scientific view of human nature confuses the relation of cause-and-effect (the influence of the past) with that of control. When a spaceship is sent to other planets, control from the Earth is unpractical. There could be a small piece of rock approaching. When it is discerned it may already be quite close. The information needs to be transmitted to the Earth. While waiting for instructions from the Earth, the probe would have been hit. Those who design a space probe need to delegate; computers in the probe will have to be programmed so that they can make their own decisions on the basis of the available information, and, if needed, change the course. Such a spaceship is granted self-control. Its programmers set up the computers in such a way that information about the environment plays a role in the control of the spaceship.

Parents do not know in what circumstances their children will find themselves. Raising them to maturity is replacing control by self-control. That this self-control is executed in a way that has been shaped by the parents, does not take away the independence of the children. This transition is not an all or nothing affair. First a child may ride her bike next to me; a few years later she may go by herself to school, and again later she may determine herself along which route to go to which destination. To some extent we can choose the environment, the friends, the schools, the books, the programmes by which we want to be influenced. We are never free in an absolute sense, as if we could start all over. It is as with reconstructing a ship at sea. You cannot take the ship apart, since you would have no place left to stand, but bit by bit you can reconstruct the ship extensively.

Sometimes a human life derails. Someone becomes addicted; 'I would like to quit, but I can't.' The choices made day-by-day – lighting another cigarette – do not fit the plan that the person would like to choose for his life. Freedom is diminished; behaviour has become compulsive. The more my acts are in line with my life plan, the more my desires for short-term pleasures are kept in check by desires about the person I would like to be, the more my acts can be considered as freely chosen.

The last word about 'free will' has not been said. I see human free will not as indeterminacy but as the remarkable fact that we humans can be guided by ideals, by a life plan. We can transcend immediate needs, desires and responses, reflect upon them, consider the circle of others concerned, and correct ourselves. Therein lies freedom. This is not unassailable; we can forego the opportunity for reflection, lose ourselves in an addiction. Evolution does not guarantee a 'happy end', not for the reindeer on St Matthew Island and the rabbits on Lisianski nor for humans on Earth. The great project of thinking and compassion on a road of freedom is a project that we have to take on, again and again. A song of praise for creation may be appropriate but there is no seventh day when the acquired treasures can be put on display in a glass case, when responsibility can be shelved.

From Now On
Playing and Imagining God

We are creatures, produced by a long history 'from nothing until now', of which we have barely begun to scratch the surface in the preceding pages. However, we are not only products but also producers. We are creative creatures; we are also looking forward, where to go 'from now on'. This creativity has a material and an intellectual form: we modify our world and ourselves, and we create our images, our understanding, both in the sciences and in religious life. In both senses, we work with our historical heritage but we are not restricted to it. We can 'play God', create new visions and new realities.

Our calling to play God

We are not only thinking beings. We are also creative creatures, beings who shape their environment. With modern technology, this has risen to unprecedented heights. In 1844 Benjamin Disraeli compared various cities to various human endeavours. Rome represents conquest, the building of empires. Jerusalem stands for faith; Athens invokes our intellectual heritage. These are the traditional examples. However, he added to this major league of human cities Manchester.

He did not add Manchester for its soccer team. Athens and Manchester stand for two different styles of human intellect, for two different styles of life, for two different dimensions of science. Astronomy is a good example of a particular kind of science, which would fit the Athenian archetype. Observations, models and theories culminate together in an understanding of many phenomena in the sky, and even in some understanding of the whole observable universe. Science is the attempt to explain, to understand reality as it is.

Manchester stands for another side of science, for the birth of chemistry and the rise of technology. This city is an archetype of the Industrial Revolution. This is science that not only seeks to understand nature, but also to create things that had not been before – a science that is not restricted to the natural but brings forth the artificial. In our days, this active, creative side of science has become enormously significant. Think of the creation of new materials with a wide variety of properties, the creation of electronics that gave rise to information and communication technologies, and of biotechnologies with major consequences for food production and medicine. Science offers more than understanding; it provides us with tools to change our world.

Technology may first be understood as '*imitating nature*', doing things which nature does as well. At some point, we move on to '*improving nature*', doing some things better than they would be done without us. 'Better' is, of course, an evaluation – and thus invites the question what the standard is by which this is judged. In what sense is our wheat after millennia of human selection 'better' than the natural varieties? Well, it is better for our purposes – for producing bread, feeding the hungry. In some contexts we may even consider ourselves to be *correcting nature*, doing things differently, averting problematic consequences of nature.

Humans are concerned about the consequences of those technologies. For physics, the archetype of responsibility has become the nuclear bomb. Chemistry is associated with pollution. Every science seems to have its particular experiences of sin, of causing problems that may be beyond its powers to solve. It is, of course, questionable whether it is science itself that is to blame, or whether one should rather blame our ways of living, our political and economic decisions. But science is involved, and this has consequences for the perception of science.

Could we and should we have done without this side of science, restricting ourselves to the noble goal of understanding? I doubt it. The active attitude is deeply rooted in human nature; we are as much *homo faber* as *homo sapiens*, and we will need both our skills and our wisdom to survive our powers, which too are in the combination of skill and intellect. Should we wish we had done without this active side, without the inventions that have changed our world? I doubt whether a moral person really can sustain such a desire. There is, of course, the mythical image of paradise, of an effortless pastoral life with fruit in abundance. If one is more realistic, we realize that we need our technology – and we need it also for morally lofty purposes, to feed the hungry, to cloth the naked, to care for those who are ill.

The lightning rod may serve as an example. In his book of over a hundred years ago, *A History of the Warfare of Science with Theology in Christendom* (1896), Andrew White dwells extensively on the resistance of church-wardens and ministers to setting up lightning rods – a resistance which not only was stupid, but immoral as it led to an unnecessarily early death of many. Frederick Ferré writes in a book titled *Hellfire and Lightning Rods* on the experiences of Swedish immigrants in Minnesota in 1922. A preacher condemned in his sermon the lightning rods, which sought to deflect the wrath of God. A young, sensitive man wondered:

> Could God's will truly be foiled by a steel rod and a grounding wire? Was it really wrong to try to protect family and livestock from the storms that swept in from the prairies with such seemingly undiscriminating force? Was God really directing the thunderbolts? Should he believe that the God Jesus called our 'Father in heaven' really would punish the farmers for taking whatever meager technological precautions might be available?

The churches have accepted the lightning rod, perhaps a few odd corners excepted. However, objections to technology surface again and again, and with them the warning that 'we should not play God' – not with medical technology, not in biotechnology. The warning against 'playing God' often indicates insecurity due to shifting boundaries between that which is given (and thus would be God's domain) and that which is in our hands to play with. Aside from the warning not 'to play God', there are also other religious images invoked in discussions on the way we humans change our world. Some invoke the notion of stewardship to express a limited, conserving range of acceptable human action. Should we limit ourselves to the role of stewards, or rather reach out as co-creators?

In the Christian tradition, the Bible is the place to look. Let me therefore offer a summary of the Bible, in a single sentence. The Bible begins on high, with paradise, which is followed by a long journey through history, with the expectation of final salvation. The combination of past *and* future returns in the liturgy in the emphasis on memory *and* hope. The Sabbath recalls the creation and the exodus and is a foretaste of fulfilment. This overarching U-shaped profile in the Christian tradition implies that images of the good are there as images of the past (paradise) and as images of the future, of a City of God, a new heaven and a new earth, the Kingdom to come. If humans are considered stewards, one looks back in time, to a good situation that has to be kept and preserved. Humans are also addressed as workers who have their eyes on the Kingdom, on that which might come.

In relation to the use of human knowledge and power, some other stories may be illuminating as well. In the synagogue Jesus meets someone with a withered hand. Will he heal on the Sabbath? Then Jesus asks: 'Is it lawful on the Sabbath to do good or to do harm, to save life or to kill?' The priority is clear. In this story of healing, from Mark 3, as in many other stories, a human is freed of the burdens of his past. A tax collector and a prostitute are again on the way of life, the possessed relax and the deaf hear. The social dimension that can also be found in the stories on the prophets, is also found in the parables. Especially those who have been less well off, get new chances; they are seen in a new light. Discipleship as serving the poor and needy has often been forgotten in Christian history, but it has resurfaced again and again. This resulted in particular in the care for orphans, widows and people who were seriously ill.

One parable explicitly speaks of stewardship (Matthew 25: 14–30). A landlord is to leave and entrusts his property to three servants. One received five talents, one two and the third only one talent, 'to each according to his ability'. The one with five talents made another five; the one with two talents made two, but the one with only one talent buried it and returned it to his master. In the end, the landlord commands that the worthless servant be cast into the outer darkness; there men will weep and gnash their teeth.

From this brief tour of biblical texts and images I conclude that in biblical language the good is not only in the past but also in the future, that humans – even when considered as stewards – can be active and even ought to be active although the initiative is with God, and that this activity is normatively determined as care for the weak and needy. Humans may not be co-creators in the sense in which God is a creator, but they are certainly *creative creatures*, or *created creators*. We are beings who genuinely act in creation, and thereby change the world and ourselves.

Stewardship has become prominent in reflection upon the ecological damage that we have done. In that context, stewardship has the connotation of nature conservation. It evokes reticence rather than the intention to change nature, but human activity is not only a threat to God's good creation. Human culture, including human technology, may also be appreciated as taking up the work God entrusted to us to work for the good. Human creativity does not diminish God. On the contrary, the more one develops one's creativity, the more one surpasses current limitations, the more God becomes God. We cannot shift the burden of responsibility to God; we are responsible. Our task becomes to make God present in the world, or, as Isabel Carter Heyward says it with a remarkable verb, our task might be 'to god the world'. The issue is that the religious sensibility not only has to do with the appreciation of beauty and goodness, but also reflects engagement with justice, with love. Transformation is a central theological theme.

Transformation as personal conversion or social change is an important theme in many theologies, especially in evangelical and political theologies. Natural theologies arising out of experiences with the natural world mostly lack this; they tend to overemphasize the way things are as deserving of wonder. However, a religiously adequate view should, in my opinion, also attempt to disclose the possibilities for transformation of the natural order. In the dialogue with the sciences, all aspects of religious faith are involved – not merely creation, but also redemption, not only 'what is' but also 'what should be'. Perhaps a complementary book to *From Nothing until Now* should be *From Now On*.

Returning to the metaphors discussed, such as stewardship and co-creator, I would stress that neither the past (images of paradise) nor the future (a new heaven and a new earth) is acceptable as the sole point of reference. It seems to me to be far more fruitful to listen to the parables and pick up the sensibility that can be found there for those in need. The question of creativity and responsibility is not whether one acts, whether one gets involved, but how – and in what way, and thus who will benefit. In that context it becomes important to be realistic about matters of power and politics, of limited knowledge and unanticipated consequences, of inequalities among humans and the even greater asymmetry between humans and other living beings. We can serve God and our neighbour with all our heart, with all our soul, with all our strength, and with all our mind – and hence also with science and technology. We may, however, be reminded that this great commandment is immediately followed (Luke 10) by the story of the Good Samaritan – thus warning us against too limited a sense of who our neighbours might be.

Creating new visions

In the course of our explorations in this book, we have seen that science offers us ideas about the world that are not directly in line with our intuitions, nor with images that have been handed down from earlier times. We humans have acquired new insights. How might this affect our faith?

'Give me that old time religion, it's good enough for me' is an appealing line in one of the spirituals. However, the 'old time religion' is challenged by new insights as well as by the recognition of so many other respectable religions on this Earth of ours. Should we not opt for a global system of ethical norms and factual beliefs, a 'naturalist religion' that could be 'everybody's story'? Should we replace the variety of religious traditions with the scientific understanding of reality?

However, religions are particular, and so are cultures, languages and individuals. Nobody speaks language; one always speaks a language. This analogy makes me wonder whether the ideal of a global, science-inspired religion is possible and desirable. Replacing all the historic languages with a single global language, whether Esperanto or English, would make much of the richness of human cultural history inaccessible. Each language allows for a slightly different angle at reality. They are not fixed, nor isolated from each other. Translations are possible even if translations never catch completely the content of the original. Languages are influenced by each other and exchange words and phrases. We cannot co-exist without interacting. We should do so, preferably, with sensitivity and respect for the variety of languages.

Similarly, different religious traditions offer different symbols, examples and ideals of a good life. One always lives within a tradition, and is at best familiar with a few traditions; human life is too short to become at home in all traditions. Thus, even when one believes that other traditions may promote rich experiences and respectable moral behaviour, one can still make a good case for raising one's children primarily with a particular set of stories, parables and commandments. To abandon the richness that is in the details of particular historical traditions for a science-based 'evolutionary epic' seems unwise. Something would be lost if the variety of religions would be replaced with a single one, whether through dominance of one particular tradition or by a 'scientific religion' invented for the purpose.

In this context, biology offers a better analogy than physics or chemistry. Diversity has arisen as the result of a long historical process with various contingencies. This rich bio-diversity is a treasure; it is to be valued. Even if one knew evolutionary theory and the conditions on Earth three billion years ago, one could not have predicted the variety of life forms that was to emerge. From a biological point of view, our understanding is encompassing, since there is no reason to assume that any of the life forms that have emerged were not the results of evolutionary processes. However, our knowledge is also limited. Not only is one unable to predict the actual variety, there are always more details than we will ever be able to explain explicitly. There is implicit wisdom in all organisms.

The variety of religious traditions, with their narratives and symbols, their rituals and exhortations, is equally impressive. Here too, much can be understood as having served biological or social functions. Here too, there may be more in the tradition than can be made explicit. The same argument applies to human nature and to human upbringing: there is more going on within us than we can make explicit or manage intentionally. If we try to replace all stories, poetry, gestures, examples and songs by explicit and univocal statements, we would lose much. Given the opaque nature of human nature, religious narratives may be considered to be valuable communicators of wisdom. Thus, 'old time religion' may be a good basis. However, we have to live with those religions in a new world, or at least, a world understood differently. Thus, we also need to understand our heritage in ways appropriate to our circumstances. Let us consider one example. If there were intelligent and sentient life elsewhere in the universe, how would that affect religious faith? In what way could the Christian tradition be modified? How do we see ourselves in this context?

Extraterrestrials may be discovered in the coming millennium. God's creation would be more abundant than previously thought. How would such a discovery affect belief in God? What would remain of the significance of Jesus, allegedly born in Bethlehem some two thousand earthly years ago? What will such a discovery do to our sense of significance?

There is a serious problem about Jesus. Philip Melanchton, a reformer with Martin Luther, wrote in 1550 that one should not imagine other inhabited worlds. It would be improper to assume that

Jesus Christ died more than once. Nor should one imagine that inhabitants of other worlds could be saved without having known the Son of God.

We might spread the Gospel via radio throughout the cosmos; quite a project for television evangelists! Not only is such a project not realistic. It is also an unsatisfactory view of faith, because religion is about the transfer of information. Would we be inspired by information about a blue person with six feet living on some planet X many light-years away? In the past millennium we have abandoned the idea that the Earth is physically the centre, but we often assume to be the centre of significance. This makes the Earth theologically unique. This is clearly the case in Christianity, where Jesus is believed to have cosmic significance.

In my opinion we need to think more modestly about Jesus. The Bible itself warns against hubris. Jesus was not born in Rome or in Jerusalem, but in Bethlehem. Not in a palace but in a stable. He is assumed to be, according to the creeds, genuinely human, flesh of our flesh and bone of our bones, as well as revelatory of God. How can we think of this revelatory role in the age of space travel and the internet? The issue is not that he provided us with new information. Faith is not about data that can be spread on the world-wide web and throughout the cosmos. The significance of his life can perhaps be expressed with a metaphor borrowed from biology. A German scholar of the New Testament, Gerd Theissen, spoke of Jesus as a mutation in cultural history. Mutations create new possibilities. The first feeble legs brought life to the land. Warm-blooded creatures could experience the cold, starry night.

Every image has its limitations. So too this image of Jesus as a mutation. Solidarity with the poor and the weak calls into question the selective process, which drives evolution. The message and example of Jesus is that in the end solidarity does more justice to reality than selection. Or, to say it in the language of faith, that God's grace is more important than God's judgment. Jesus goes against the exclusion of strangers. He speaks of love for one's enemy. At the cross, the helpless one is claimed to be Lord of All, the victim is the priest.

What about persons on other planets? They will not know of incarnation or crucifixion. They will not have a Bible in Hebrew and Greek. There will not be a story about someone who has been beaten on the road from Jericho to Jerusalem – and then is helped by a stranger rather than by a priest of his own tribe. It could be, however, that the idea of love has been radicalized there too. That they too have, in their better moments, the sense that one should love not only one's family or friends, that even the stranger and the enemy should be seen as neighbours. There will be no story of a son who has spoilt his inheritance and has to take care of pigs, but there may well be a message of forgiveness. There might be stories of making a new beginning – just as 'the lost son' could return home. The language and the images will be quite different. Convictions and values will be different too. At the same time, one may hope for a deeper affinity.

A lover says 'You are the loveliest' without making a cosmic claim. One travels with one's beloved in trust and love – but one has not made an investigation, on Earth and beyond, to justify the claim 'You are the loveliest.' So too will religious language always be close to our hearts. We will have a particular story as the most important one. Jesus Christ can well be the centre of our faith, of our lives. Whatever our tradition, it is more important to be open minded, loving and responsible, than to include extraterrestrials in traditional theological schemes.

Extraterrestrial company is a challenge for Christian theology. This challenge should be welcomed. Just as we do not like to be accused of racism or sexism, so too will 'planetism' be unacceptable. If we ever get into contact – which may not be soon or easy, given the huge distances – we cannot assume to be closer to God than they are.

Let me return from this example to the more general issue. What might be the best way to proceed with images and concepts offered by religious traditions as part of our heritage? I do think that the development of physics offers a helpful analogy.

When we consider major transitions, such as those from Newton's ideas about space and time to Einstein's views, or from classical to quantum conceptions of matter, we may be struck by the newness of the concepts involved. There seems to be no continuity in the way reality is seen, that is, in ontology. However, there is continuity at less abstract levels of knowing, for instance with respect to predictions for the orbits of planets. The way from the older to the newer view is not via a translation at the level of theories. Rather, new theories are proposed, creatively. However, new theories have to do justice to the experiences and experiments coded and covered in the old theories.

Similarly in religion. Continuity with the insights of earlier humans, including those found in the Bible and the writings of the early churches, should be sought at the level of life as lived. The more abstract levels, including notions such as the trinity, the virgin birth, heaven, and even God, are constructions, and such constructions or interpretations may change drastically even though one seeks to be fair to the underlying experiences. Fundamentalists and those who reject Christianity because they think it has to be fundamentalist, often make the error of conflating different levels. They take the original expressions to be as important as the underlying experiences and concerns themselves.

Thus, in my view the best way to renew religious language and models is to consider how those images functioned for humans in earlier periods, and to find out as far as possible what the underlying concerns and experiences were. In as far as we recognize those experiences and concerns and see them as our own, we can attempt to develop new images and models, new ways of dealing with them in images which are credible in our time, in the context of all else that we take seriously, including science. Rather than focussing on the truth claims embodied in metaphors and models, I prefer to give primacy to the relevance these images had in the context of the period.

Wandering humans

Religious traditions are complex entities. Each one offers a particular language, with certain metaphors and concepts. A way of life may be suggested by parables, as for instance that of the good Samaritan helping a stranger from another culture (Luke 10: 29–37), by historical narratives, such as various accounts of prophets protesting against injustice or of Jesus forgiving those who persecuted him, and it may be articulated in commandments, such as the Ten Commandments (Deuteronomy 5: 6–21). Such a way of life need not always strengthen the conformity of the believer to the expectations of the larger community; it may also emphasize individual responsibility even where the individual goes counter to the interests of others. Such a way of life is not only a practical matter. It is oriented by an ultimate ideal that surpasses any actual achievable goal or situation. Thus, religious traditions include elements such as 'the Kingdom', 'Paradise', 'Heaven', 'Nirvana', immortality, emptiness, openness, perfection, or unconditional love. Such notions function as ideals against which actual behaviour is contrasted in order to evaluate it. A tradition's way of life is affirmed and strengthened by the particular forms of worship and devotion of that religious tradition. Worship and other forms of ritual behaviour express and nourish the individual and communal spirituality in relation to the joys, sorrows, and challenges of life, and to the conceptions and ultimate ideals of good life.

Religious variety is acceptable, natural, and valuable. The variety of ways of life may well be a rich resource and a colourful element in our own time. Variety is to be expected, since we deal with human experiences (of various kinds in a wide variety of contexts), and different forms of ritual behaviour and different guiding ideals of human flourishing may be entertained. However, no tradition is beyond dispute and beyond development. There is no reason to dismiss at once such complex cultural entities as religious traditions as being at odds with natural science, but neither do we have to accept our own tradition, or any other, without critical scrutiny nor as a yes-or-no package deal. Change is characteristic of our history, and there is no need to exclude religious traditions from it.

Our circumstances change, as do our moral and spiritual sensitivities, for example with respect to conflicts between ethnic or religious groups, slavery, or cruelty to animals. Religious traditions, changing circumstances, a wider encounter with other cultures, and philosophical insights have contributed to this process of change. One more challenge resulting in change, but not the most important one, is the credibility of a tradition. If the images supporting the way of life are not recognizable, or if the claims by which the way of life is justified have become incredible, that too challenges the religious tradition, though more indirectly than challenges to the appropriateness of the circumstances of the way of life and to its moral and spiritual adequacy.

Granted that we may have to discard some traditions or may have to modify them, why would one keep alive any such tradition? The reason is, in my opinion, that they are useful and powerful. They are useful and powerful, not only for unreflective moments and persons, but also for reflective and well-informed persons. No human is only a rational being who could entertain all his motives and desires consciously and intentionally; the structure of our brains is such that much goes on which is not dealt with consciously. This is the risk involved in religious forms of behaviour (since so much cannot be scrutinized consciously) and the reason for their importance: through religious metaphors and forms of behaviour we address reality especially in a way which confronts us with ideals, with what ought to be, with a vision of a better world, or with images of a paradisiacal past or an ultimate comforting presence.

Wondering humans

Religious traditions have another dimension too. Humans have, with the development of consciousness and communication, contemplated questions about the world in which they found themselves. Creation myths may well have been functional, ways of presenting and justifying moral imperatives and social structures. However, the myths also play with the possibilities of thinking, or at least reach beyond what is sufficient for the circumstances of the moment. In earlier ages, answers to speculative questions may have been closely allied with the way the world was experienced, which is still to a large extent reflected in our manifest image of the world. In this manifest image, persons are the major agents from which action proceeds. Hence, it is not very amazing that animist ways of speaking about the world have become widespread; experiences with many phenomena are modelled after experiences with human agents. Sometimes, such agents are understood as residing in the phenomena, say as spirits, and sometimes, the agent is thought of as a god who transcends the phenomena but acts through them.

Such models are still with us; animist ways of speaking about cars or computers are common, and many persons discern intentions behind bad luck such as being struck by a disease. I consider the belief in such intentions a remnant of earlier times when manifest ways of speaking were not yet corrected through the development of scientific images; such ways of speaking and thinking are interesting as phenomena but they are not credible given our knowledge of cars and cancers. However, even though earlier answers have lost their credibility and questions may have changed their appearance, humans can still be wondering persons, contemplating questions that transcend our current answers. Religious traditions offer answers to such questions, but – more importantly, in my view – they are thereby also ways of posing such questions, and thus ways of nourishing sensitivity to such questions. Maintaining this speculative openness is one role of limit questions.

The openness expressed in the limit questions may induce a sense of wonder and gratitude about the reality to which we belong. Such a cosmological approach might primarily be at home with a mystical form of religion, a sense of unity and belonging, as well as dependence upon something surpassing our world.

We know, collectively, a great deal about our world. Our knowledge is also limited. Certain phenomena may be intractable, even though they fit into the naturalist framework. And limit questions regarding the whole naturalist framework can be posed but will not be answered. In a book of aphorisms, *The Aristos*, the novelist John Fowles has given a positive appreciation of such limitations to our knowledge.

> We are in the best possible situation because everywhere, below the surface, we do not know; we shall never know why; we shall never know tomorrow; we shall never know a god or if there is a god; we shall never even know ourselves. This mysterious wall round our world and our perception of it is not there to frustrate us but to train us back to the now, to life, to our time being.

I wonder how Fowles knows that we shall never know. He even knows why we do not know: to train us back to life! 'To train us back to life': the notion of such a purpose of our limitations is inadequate; it has simply happened that we are endowed with our capacities and our limitations. However, the emphasis on the wider context of knowledge, our lives, fits well.

> *Our knowledge and our capacity for knowledge have arisen in the midst of life, and if we are to use them anywhere at all, it will have to be there. They allow us to wonder about that which transcends and sustains our reality, but all the time we wander in the reality in which we live, move, and have our being; to its future we contribute our lives.*

Notes and literature

General

The views presented here have been developed in greater detail in my *Beyond the Big Bang: Quantum Cosmologies and God* (La Salle, IL: Open Court, 1990) and in my *Religion, Science and Naturalism* (Cambridge: Cambridge University Press, 1996), as well as in contributions to various books and journals, e.g. in Niels Henrik Gregersen and Wentzel J. van Huyssteen (eds) *Rethinking Theology and Science: Six Models for the Current Dialogue* (Grand Rapids, MI: Eerdmans, 1998), in R. J. Russell *et al.* (eds) *Evolutionary and Molecular Biology: Scientific Perspectives on Divine Action* (Vatican City: Vatican Observatory and Berkeley: Center for Theology and the Natural Sciences, 1998), and in articles on 'naturalism' in *Zygon: Journal of Religion and Science* in December 1997, 1998 and 2000. An earlier version of this book appeared in Dutch as *Van Niets tot Nu: Een wetenschappelijke scheppingsvertelling* (Kampen: Kok, 1996). Klaus Blömer translated the book into German, where it appeared in an expanded form as *Vom Nichts zum Jetzt: Eine etwas andere Schöpfungsgeschichte* (Hannover: Lutherisches Verlagshaus, 1998). An earlier and briefer version of the creation narrative and its explication appeared as the first of two Andreas Idreos lectures, held in May 1998 (Oxford: Harris Manchester College).

There are many good, interesting books on the relations between religion and science. I recommend Arthur Peacocke's *Theology for a Scientific Age: Being and Becoming – Natural, Divine and Human,* enlarged edn (London: SCM, 1993) and his *Creation and the World of Science* (Oxford: Clarendon Press, 1979). A reliable guide is also Ian Barbour's *Religion and Science: Historical and Contemporary*

Issues (San Francisco: Harper, 1997). *God, Humanity and the Cosmos: A Textbook in Science and Religion*, Christopher Southgate *et al.* (eds) (Edinburgh: T & T Clark, 1999) is aimed primarily at students and teachers. On monotheism in relation to evolution there is an intriguing book by the New Testament scholar Gerd Theissen, *Biblical Faith: An Evolutionary Approach* (London: SCM, 1985). The evolution of humans and human cultures is the focus of Philip Hefner's *The Human Factor: Evolution, Culture and Religion* (Minneapolis: Fortress, 1993). Other wide-ranging and interesting theological proposals are, in my opinion, John Hick, *An Interpretation of Religion: Human Responses to the Transcendent* (Basingstoke: Macmillan, 1989), which considers various religions as different responses to one Reality; and Gordon Kaufman, *In Face of Mystery: A Constructive Theology* (Cambridge, MA: Harvard University Press, 1993), which underlines the creativity of the evolutionary process and the importance of regulative ideals. A study of Biblical material which has inspired me is Samuel Terrien, *The Elusive Presence: Toward a New Biblical Theology* (San Francisco: Harper & Row, 1978).

There are many excellent books to inform the lay reader (and the scientist from a different discipline) on developments in various disciplines. In the following, I have often referred to articles from *Scientific American* and some of the popular science literature; they provide access to the wealth of secondary and primary literature on these issues. The main title resembles Peter W. Atkins's *The Creation* (Oxford: Freeman and Co., 1981), a book that is mainly focused on issues of 'ultimate explanation'. Despite significant differences in style, content, and main thesis, I highly appreciate Atkins's engagement, communicative skills, and scientific acumen.

Introduction

pp. 2–3 There are various other contemporary articulations and imaginations of our place in reality, such as the novel by Franco Ferrucci, *The Life of God: As Told by Himself* (Chicago: University of Chicago Press, 1997) and the poems by the Dutch-American biochemist Leo Vroman, e.g. in *Love, Greatly Enlarged* (Merrick, NY: Cross-Cultural Communications). In *The Sacred Depths of Nature* (Oxford: Oxford University Press, 1998) the biologist Ursula Goodenough offers a series of inspiring vignettes, which are to a large extent rooted in cell biology. Brian Swimme, *The Hidden Heart of the Cosmos: Humanity and the New Story* (Maryknoll, NY: Orbis Books, 1996) comes to the enterprise of rethinking our place and responsibility from cosmology. Matthew Fox, *Creation Spirituality: Liberating Gifts for the Peoples of the Earth* (New York: HarperCollins, 1991) also integrates narrative and argument, though the sciences play less of a role. Thomas Berry, *The Great Work: Our Way into the Future* (New York: Bell Tower, 1999) is another example of 'big history', told in order to underline our responsibility. A more theoretical articulation of 'big history' is offered by Fred Spier, *The Structure of Big History: From the Big Bang until Today* (Amsterdam: Amsterdam University Press, 1996). A readable overview of human history in ecological perspective is Jared Diamond's *Guns, Germs and Steel: A Short History of Everybody over the Last 13,000 Years* (London: Random House, Vintage, 1998). More wide ranging is *A Walk Through Time: From Stardust to Us*, by Sidney Liebes, Elisabeth Santouris and Brian Swimme (New York: John Wiley and Sons, 1998). Arthur Peacocke has offered his poetic rendering of the Christian creation story in the modern cosmological and evolutionary context in an article in *Zygon: Journal of Religion and Science* 34 (December 1999), 695–712, see especially p. 696.

p. 3 Scholars and scientists, conferences: I have benefited greatly from time at the Center for Theology and the Natural Sciences in Berkeley, the Chicago Center for Religion and Science (since renamed the Zygon Center for Religion and Science), and the Center for Theological Inquiry in Princeton. Enriching has also been the opportunity to participate in three conferences organized by the Center for Theology and the Natural Sciences and the Vatican Observatory, the January workshops of the Ian Ramsey Centre in Oxford, and invitations to numerous lectures in Europe, Canada and the United States. Last but not least two organizations have been very important to me. The European Society for the Study of Science and Theology (ESSSAT) which organizes an open conference every two years where scientists, philosophers and theologians from all over Europe as well as from other continents meet; and IRAS, the Institute on Religion in an Age of Science, founded in 1954, which holds its annual conferences on Star Island near Portsmouth, NH.

Scene 1. When time was not yet

p. 9 For the history of astronomy, a practical resource is John North, *The Fontana History of Astronomy* (London: Fontana Press, 1994; US edition as *The Norton History of Astronomy*). Accessible is Marcelo Gleiser, *The Dancing Universe: From Creation Myths to the Big Bang* (New York: Penguin, 1997), which pays a lot of attention to the long road towards human understanding, from various creation myths and the Greeks through the rise of modern science, until the Big Bang theory. Informative and highly readable, with a nice historical introduction as well as recent developments, is Heinz Pagels, *Perfect Symmetry: The Search for the Beginning of Time* (New York: Simon and Schuster, 1985).

p.10 Olbers's paradox: see North *The Fontana History of Astronomy*, among others.

p. 11 Aurelius Augustine, *Confessiones*, Book Eleven (XIII, 15). That time depends on movement was the view already held by Aristotle, centuries earlier.

pp. 12–13 Stephen Hawking, *A Brief History of Time* (New York: Bantam Books, 1988); see also John D. Barrow, *The Origin of the Universe* (London: Weidenfeld & Nicolson, 1994). Chris J. Isham offers substantial informative reflections on time in quantum cosmology in contributions to *Physics, Philosophy and Theology: A Common Quest for Understanding*, R. J. Russell, W. R. Stoeger, G. V. Coyne (eds) (Vatican City: Vatican Observatory, 1988), pp. 375–408; and *Quantum Cosmologies and the Laws of Nature: Scientific Perspectives on Divine Action*, R. J. Russell, N. Murphy, C. J. Isham (eds) (Vatican City: Vatican Observatory and Berkeley: Center for Theology and the Natural Sciences, 1993), pp. 49–89. I wrote more extensively on these issues in the later volume (pp. 331–365) and in my *Beyond the Big Bang* (pp. 41–75). A strong advocate of a non-temporal understanding of reality (with temporal processes, and thus history, as a secondary rather than a fundamental aspect) is Julian Barbour, *The End of Time: The Next Revolution in Our Understanding of the Universe* (London: Weidenfeld & Nicolson, 1999). One of the ideas which currently attracts a lot of interest is the concept of 'superstrings', which would not only affect our understanding of matter (as vibrations of strings rather than as point particles) but also of space and time. See, for a wide-ranging presentation, Brian Greene, *The Elegant Universe: Superstrings,*

Hidden Dimensions, and the Quest for the Ultimate Theory (New York: Norton, 1999); also 'The Theory Formerly Known as Strings', by Michael J. Duff, *Scientific American* 278 (February 1998), pp. 54–59. For new observational developments in cosmology and their consequences, see the report 'Brave New Cosmos' in *Scientific American* 284 (January 2001), pp. 27–47.

Scene 2. Mystery

p. 14–15 The image of passing on questions has been taken from Charles W. Misner, 'Cosmology and Theology', in *Cosmology, History and Theology*, W. Yourgrau, A. D. Breck (eds) (New York: Plenum Press, 1977), p. 97. Steven Weinberg used it in a similar way in his *Dreams of a Final Theory: The Search for the Fundamental Laws of Nature* (New York: Pantheon Books, 1992), p. 242.

pp. 15–17 A major study on the anthropic principles is John D. Barrow, Frank J. Tipler, *The Anthropic Cosmological Principle* (Oxford: Clarendon Press, 1986). A universe with the mass of a single galaxy is considered on pages 384ff. My objections to arguments based on the anthropic coincidences can be found in *Beyond the Big Bang*, pp. 78–89. 'The anthropomurphic principle' (our universe being precisely fine-tuned for Murphy's law to hold, so that, for instance, buttered toast falls upside-down on the floor) is considered in *Scientific American* 273 (December 1995), pp. 86f. by Ian Stewart and, more extensively, 276 (April 1997), pp. 72–75 by Robert A. J. Matthews.

p. 17 A careful analysis of inflationary models in cosmology, with references to all major articles, is John Earman and Jesus Mosterin, 'A Critical Look at Inflationary Cosmology', *Philosophy of Science* 66 (March 1999), pp. 1–49.

p. 19 Misner, 'Cosmology and Theology', p. 96.

Scene 3. Integrity

pp. 21–22 The notions of symmetry and asymmetry are discussed well in Frank Close, *Lucifer's Legacy: The Meaning of Asymmetry* (Oxford: Oxford University Press, 2000); the example of the Indonesian Sultan buying a British car, and thus setting Indonesia on the course of left-hand driving, can be found on page 44.

Symmetry and symmetry-breaking in physics and cosmology is also explicated clearly in Heinz R. Pagels, *Perfect Symmetry*, Gerard 't Hooft, *In Search of the Ultimate Building Blocks of Creation* (Cambridge, Cambridge University Press, 1996), Steven Weinberg, *Dreams of a Final Theory*, and in many other informative books on fundamental physics and cosmology.

p. 23 That the total energy of the universe might be zero has been proposed by E. P. Tryon, 'Is the Universe a Vacuumfluctation?', *Nature* 246 (1973), pp. 396–397.

p. 25 John Fowles, *The Aristos* (Falmouth: Granada, 1981) p. 27.

Scene 4. Dependence

p. 27 *The First Three Minutes* is the title of a book by the cosmologist Steven Weinberg (New York: Basic Books, 1977). For a popular book it has been exceptionally influential within the discipline by stimulating the merger of cosmology and elementary particle physics.

Scene 5. Purpose

p. 29 The quote from Mark Twain is taken from Stephen J. Gould, *Wonderful Life: The Burgess Shale and the Nature of History* (New York: Norton, 1989), p. 45.

p. 30 An 'historical' understanding of function is argued for by Ruth G. Millikan in her *Language, Thought and Other Biological Categories* (Cambridge, MA: MIT Press, 1984); and in her *White Queen Psychology and Other Essays for Alice* (Cambridge, MA: MIT Press, 1989); see also Anne Ruth Mackor, 'The Alleged Autonomy of Psychology and the Social Sciences', in *Logic and Philosophy of Science in Uppsala*, D. Prawitz, D. Westerståhl (eds) (Dordrecht: Kluwer, 1994).

p. 31 George C. Williams, *Plan and Purpose in Nature* (London: Weidenfeld & Nicolson, 1996), p. 13, discusses the nerves of the eye including the problem of a detached retina; see also, on the eye, R. Dawkins, *Climbing Mount Improbable* (London: Penguin, 1996), pp. 126–129. Evolution not only applies to humans and furry animals, but also makes diseases intelligible; see Randolph M. Nesse and George C. Williams, 'Evolution and the Origins of Disease',

Scientific American 279 (November 1998), pp. 58–65. The basic evolutionary insight is that the human body, and any other organism, is a bundle of compromises, since there are often trade-offs between various features and also historical 'hang-ups'.

Scene 6. Luck

pp. 33–34 On the evolution of the atmosphere, see C. J. Allègre and S. H. Schneider, 'The Evolution of the Earth', *Scientific American* 271 (October 1994), pp. 44–51. This is an issue on 'Life in the Universe' which has various other useful articles as well. On contemporary challenges, see for instance John T. Houghton, *Global Warming: The Complete Briefing*, 2nd edn (Cambridge: Cambridge University Press, 1997).

p. 35 On the origin of the eukaryotic cell, an introduction with further references by 1974 Nobel Prize winner Christian De Duve, 'The Birth of Complex Cells' in *Scientific American* 274 (April 1996), pp. 38–45; the quote about enslavement is from page 45. A more complicated understanding of the early, unicellular stages of 'the tree of life', with gene-transfer between branches of bacteria, archae and eukaryotes has been presented by W. Ford Doolittle, 'Uprooting the Tree of Life', *Scientific American* 282 (February 2000), pp. 72–77.

pp. 35–36 On planets with other stars, J. R. P. Angel and N. J. Woolf, 'Searching for Life on Other Planets', *Scientific American* 274 (April 1996): pp. 46–52. 'The Case for Relic Life on Mars' is an essay by members of the team that claimed indications of microbial extraterrestrial life from Mars in a meteorite, *Scientific American* 277 (December 1997), pp. 36–41.

pp. 36–40 S. J. Gould stresses in his book *Wonderful Life* the many contingencies in evolutionary history; the quote is from page 291. The classification of fossils to which he appeals, has since been revised; there may well be much less diversity; see Conway Morris, *The Crucible of Creation: The Burgess Shale and the Rise of Animals* (Oxford: Oxford University Press, 1998), and, more popular, the criticisms by Daniel C. Dennett in *Darwin's Dangerous Idea: Evolution and the Meanings of Life* (New York: Simon and Schuster, 1995). Morris, Dennett, and others emphasize convergence, the emergence in different evolutionary lineages of similar adaptations to an environment. Ernst Mayr, *Toward a New Philosophy of*

Biology: Observations of an Evolutionist (Cambridge, MA: Harvard University Press, 1988), p. 72, emphasizes that convergence, together with the observation that our kind of intelligence has arisen only once on Earth, supports the conviction that the probability of intelligence on other life-bearing planets is low (per planet). That is the line taken in the text, even though the use of statistics to prove this is problematic. Though contact seems unlikely, given distances and time delays involved, we should in principle be open to the possibility of sentient life elsewhere. I discussed the theological implications, in Dutch, in *Tijdschrift voor Theologie* 27 (1987), pp. 259–276, and, briefly, in Russell Stannard (ed.) *God for the 21st Century* (Philadelphia: Templeton Foundation Press, 2000; see also in the current book the final section 'From now on', esp. pp. 90–92). 'Extraterrestrial life' has always been a fascinating area of speculation, reflecting views of human nature and possibilities, as covered very well in Stephen J. Dick, *Plurality of Worlds: The Origins of the Extraterrestrial Life Debate from Democritus to Kant* (1982); Michael J. Crowe, *The Extraterrestrial Life Debate, 1750–1900: The Idea of a Plurality of Worlds from Kant to Lowell* (1986) and S. J. Dick, *The Biological Universe: The Twentieth-Century Extraterrestrial Life Debate and the Limits of Science* (1996) – all published by Cambridge University Press.

Scene 7. Humanity

p. 41 Jared Diamond, *The Rise and Fall of the Third Chimpanzee* (London: Random House, 1991). On bonobos and chimpanzees, see for instance Frans de Waal, 'Bonobo Sex and Society', *Scientific American* 272 (March 1995): pp. 58–64; and his *Good Natured: The Origins of Right and Wrong in Humans and Other Animals* (Cambridge, MA: Harvard University Press, 1996).

pp. 42–44 For a good overview see Camilio Cela-Conde, 'The Hominid Evolutionary Journey', in *Evolutionary and Molecular Biology: Scientific Perspectives on Divine Action*, R. J. Russell, W. R. Stoeger, F. J. Ayala (eds) (Vatican City: Vatican Observatory, and Berkeley: Center for Theology and the Natural Sciences, 1998), pp. 59–79. 'Once We Were not Alone' by Ian Tattersall in *Scientific American* 282 (January 2000), pp. 38–44, documents the variety of cousins that there have been in and around the hominid lineage. 'Out of Africa Again . . . and Again?' by Ian Tattersall in *Scientific*

American 276 (April 1997), pp. 46–53) argues in favour of various migrations out of Africa over the last few million years. William Calvin argues in *The Ascent of Mind: Ice Age Climates and the Evolution of Intelligence* for the significance of the pressures of subarctic existence for the rise of human intelligences. For the capacities of Neanderthals I follow Cela-Conde; a mostly positive account is also Kate Wing, 'Who Were the Neanderthals?', *Scientific American* 282 (April 2000), pp. 78–87, who also considers the case for a biological contribution of Neanderthals to European ancestry. Diamond puts more emphasis on the difference from our immediate ancestors. De Waal, *Good Natured*, discusses for other species examples of the survival of handicapped individuals comparable to the hominid found in La Chapelle aux Saints. The term 'East Side Story' has been taken from Y. Coppens, 'East Side Story: The Origin of Human Kind', *Scientific American* 270 (May 1994): pp. 62–69.

pp. 45–47 On indirect reciprocity, see Richard Alexander, *The Biology of Moral Systems* (New York: De Gruyter, 1987). Group selection has recently been articulated and defended by D. S. Wilson and E. Sober, 'Reintroducing Group Selection to the Human Behavioral Sciences', *Behavioral and Brain Sciences* 17 (1994), pp. 585–654; see also their book *Unto Others: The Evolution and Psychology of Unselfish Behavior* (Cambridge, MA: Harvard University Press, 1998). See also De Waal, *Good Natured*; essays by Michael Ruse, Francisco Ayala and Elliott Sober in *Biology, Ethics and the Origins of Life*, Holmes Rolston (ed.) (Boston: Jones and Bartlett, 1995); and essays in *Evolutionary Ethics*, M. H. Nitecki and D. V. Nitecki (eds) (Albany, NY: SUNY Press, 1993). On the role of reflection and public justification, see among others Philip Kitcher, *Vaulting Ambition: Sociobiology and the Quest for Human Nature* (Cambridge, MA: MIT Press, 1985) and Peter Singer, *The Expanding Circle: Ethics and Sociobiology* (Oxford: Clarendon Press, 1981) as well as the more recent 'manifesto' by Peter Singer, *A Darwinian Left: Politics, Evolution and Cooperation* (London: Weidenfeld & Nicolson, 1999). This emphasis on reflection is not to deny the role of emotions; see Antonio R. Damasio, *Descartes' Error: Emotion, Reason and the Human Brain* (New York: Putnam, 1994).

pp. 47–49 There is currently an extensive literature on the philosophy of mind. An interesting example is Terrence Deacon, *The Symbolic Species: The Co-evolution of Language and the Human*

Brain (London: Penguin Books, 1997). I have learned much from discussions resulting in Willem B. Drees (ed.) *De mens: Meer dan materie?* (Kampen: Kok, 1997), and especially from the essay by T. Bas Jongeling, 'Wat is reductionisme?' which emphasizes the role of the desired, constructed isomorphy between the material (syntactic) process and the semantic connections. This was also refered to in my review article 'God and Contemporary Science: Philip Clayton's Defense of Panentheism', *Zygon: Journal of Religion and Science* 34 (September 1999), pp. 515–525. J. Schwartz distinguishes various kinds of reductionism in a helpful way in his 'Reductionism, Elimination, and the Mental', *Philosophy of Science* 58 (1991), pp. 203–220.

Scene 8. Religion

pp. 50–52 Ralph W. Burhoe, *Towards a Scientific Theology* (Belfast: Christian Journals, 1981), founder of the journal *Zygon: Journal of Religion and Science*, has defended forcefully that religion has been an essential element in the evolutionary history of humanity by supporting the cooperation within larger groups of non-kin. Such a 'biocultural' approach to religion is quite prominent in *Zygon*; see also Philip Hefner, *The Human Factor*, its current editor in chief.

pp. 51–52 J. Diamond, *The Rise and Fall of the Third Chimpanzee*, chapter 10, discusses ambivalences related to the rise of agriculture. Cain as the ancestor of wandering pastors, musicians and smiths: see Genesis 4: 20–22. Canaites or Kenites are mentioned in Judges 1: 16 and 4: 11. Dietrich Ritschl, *Zur Logik der Theologie* (München: Kaiser, 1984), p. 34, sees religions as a response to stress, dependencies and hierarchical relations related to the new style of life.

pp. 52–53 The 'Axial Age' has been emphasized by John Hick in his *An Interpretation of Religion* and by Karen Armstrong, *A History of God. From Abraham to the Present: The 4000 Year Quest for God* (London: William Heinemann, 1993); the concept originates with Karl Jaspers.

pp. 53–54 The parable of the Good Samaritan can be found in Luke 10: 25–37. A speculative but interesting interpretation of Jesus in relation to developments in Jewish monotheism is offered by Gerd Theissen, *Biblischer Glaube aus evolutionärer Sicht* (München: Kaiser, 1984); translated as *Biblical Faith*.

INTERMEZZO: THE NATURE OF THEOLOGY

pp. 54–56 The philosopher of religion John Hick (*An Interpretation of Religion*) has granted prominence to the ambiguity of our knowledge, especially when it comes to ideas about God, especially in the part on 'The religious ambiguity of the universe'.

pp. 56–57 Samuel Terrien, *The Elusive Presence* discusses the passages refered to in more detail. That one might say of the biblical God that 'as Lord he might be servant, in smallness great' has been appropriated from H. G. Hubbeling who describes in his *Philosophy of Religion* (Assen: Van Gorcum, 1987), p. 79, that upon the view of the theologian Karl Barth 'the decisive characteristic of the biblical God is that he, as Lord, can at the same time be a servant. He can be great even in his smallness, he can be majestic, even in his humiliation.' On Xenophanes, see H. Diels, *Die Fragmente der Vorsokratiker*, 2nd edn (Berlin: Weidman, 1906–1910), I, 15 and 23.

p. 58 Post-biblical negative theology: J. Hochstaffl, *Negative Theologie* (München: Kösel Verlag, 1976), 82–155.

p. 58–60 The definition by Geertz can be found in 'Religion as a Cultural System', in Clifford Geertz, *The Interpretation of Cultures* (New York: Basic Books, 1973), p. 90. For an exemplary study of the moral roles of creation myths situated in an historical or mythical past, see R. W. Lovin and F. E. Reynolds (eds) *Cosmogony and Ethical Order: New Studies in Comparative Ethics* (Chicago: University of Chicago Press, 1985).

p. 60 The quotes from William James, *The Varieties of Religious Experience*, of which there are many editions, have been taken from Lecture 2. Fritjof Capra, *The Turning Point* (New York: Simon and Schuster, 1982).

Scene 9. Critical thought

pp. 62–63 H. Floris Cohen, *The Scientific Revolution: A Historiographical Inquiry* (Chicago: University of Chicago Press, 1994) discusses various views of the causes for the Scientific Revolution. Earlier developments are described by David C. Lindberg in *The Beginnings of Western Science: The European Scientific Tradition in Philosophical, Religious and Institutional*

Context, 600 BC to AD 1450 (Chicago: University of Chicago Press, 1992).

p. 64 The formulation on Enlightenment by Immanuel Kant is from his article 'Beantwortung der Frage: Was ist Aufklärung?' (1784).

INTERMEZZO: THE NATURE OF KNOWLEDGE

pp. 65–69 That even within a modest, constructive view of scientific knowledge one can speak of advancement has been argued, convincingly in my opinion, by Philip Kitcher in his book *The Advancement of Science* (New York: Oxford University Press, 1993). The various characteristics of science and the difference between scientific and manifest images have been discussed at greater length in my *Religion, Science and Naturalism*, pp. 6–10. Among the critical studies refuting creationist and similar abuse of recent insights from the philosophy and history of science, there are Philip Kitcher, *Abusing Science: The Case Against Creationism* (Cambridge, MA: MIT Press, 1982); Michael Ruse (ed.) *But is it Science?* (Buffalo: Prometheus Books, 1996); a chapter in Elliott Sober, *Philosophy of Biology*, 2nd edn (Westview Press, 2000); and Robert T. Pennock, *Tower of Babel: The Evidence against the New Creationism* (Cambridge, MA: MIT Press, 1999). On some related issues see also articles by N. Shanks and K. H. Joplin, 'Redundant Complexity: A Critical Analysis of Intelligent Design in Biochemistry', *Philosophy of Science* 66 (June 1999), pp. 268–282; and by B. Fitelson, C. Stephens, E. Sober, *Philosophy of Science* 66 (September 1999), pp. 472–488; as well as by Howard J. Van Till, 'Does "Intelligent Design" have a chance? An essay review', *Zygon: Journal of Religion and Science* 34 (December 1999), pp. 667–676.

INTERMEZZO: OUR KNOWLEDGE OF NATURE

pp. 69–76 My understanding of 'naturalism' is presented, in contrast with other ways of understanding naturalism and with a variety of references, in *Religion, Science and Naturalism*, pp. 10–23, and in 'Naturalisms and Religion', in *Zygon: Journal of Religion and Science* 22 (December 1997), pp. 525–541. The open-ended character of naturalism which allows for a theistic, a pantheistic or an agnostic response, is articulated in 'Should Religious Naturalists Promote a Naturalistic Religion?', also in *Zygon* 33 (December 1998), pp. 617–633.

p. 70 John Fowles, *The Tree* (St Albans: Sumach, 1979), pp. 40f.

pp. 71–75 On varieties of reductionism and the difference with elimination, see J. Schwartz, 'Reduction, Elimination and the Mental', *Philosophy of Science* 58 (1991): pp. 203–220.

pp. 75–76 On the difference between argumentative and narrative styles, see Jerome Bruner, *Actual Minds, Possible Worlds* (Cambridge, MA: Harvard University Press, 1986), p. 11. Bas C. van Fraassen is quoted from his essay 'The World of Empiricism', in J. Hilgevoord (ed.) *Physics and Our View of the World* (Cambridge: Cambridge University Press, 1994), p. 133.

Scene 10. Responsibility

p. 78 Antonio Damasio, *Descartes' Error* is one of many who emphasize that bodily, biological existence is the basis for feeling and thinking, rather than inhibitive to it.

pp. 78–80 Infanticide and genocide by humans and by apes is discussed by J. Diamond, *The Rise and Fall of the Third Chimpanzee*, chapter 16. On violence among Apes and the emotional resistance against accepting this view of our nearest relatives there is the novel *Brazzaville Beach* by William Boyd (1990). The examples of ecological destruction by humans, reindeer and rabbits have been taken from J. Diamond (chapters 17–19). C. N. Runnels, 'Environmental Degradation in Ancient Greece', *Scientific American* 272 (March 1995): pp. 72–75, discusses earlier ecologically self-destructive behaviour of humans. See W. S. Broecker, 'Chaotic Climate', *Scientific American* 273 (November 1995): pp. 44–50, on the role of major streams in the oceans on the global climate. As he sees it, the climate has been remarkably stable over the last ten-thousand years; in other epochs there may have been changes in average temperature of the order of ten degrees Celsius within a period of ten years or so. The possibility that the warm Gulf Stream might reverse is, among many others, discussed in William Calvin, *The Ascent of Mind*. For a sobering view of the evolutionary origins of our spiritual and rational powers, which allowed us to (over)populate and dominate the earth, and thereby led us to the brink of extinction (corresponding, roughly speaking, to scenes 7–10), see Reg Morrison, *The Spirit in the Gene: Humanity's Proud Illusion and the Laws of Nature* (Ithaca: Cornell University Press, 1999).

pp. 80–81 On utopian thought and the distinction between a technical and a social utopia I have learned much from Hans J. Achterhuis, *De erfenis van de utopie* (Amsterdam: Boom, 1998).

pp. 81–83 On free will, examples of compatibilists are Daniel C. Dennett, *Elbow Room: The Varieties of Free Will Worth Wanting* (Cambridge, MA: MIT Press, 1984), which develops the analogy of the spaceship extensively, and Hilary Bok, *Freedom and Responsibility* (Princeton, NJ: Princeton University Press, 1998); see also Mary Midgley, *The Human Primate: Humans, Freedom and Morality* (London: Routledge, 1994). Robert Kane, *The Significance of Free Will* (Oxford: Oxford University Press, 1996) has articulated well a non-compatibilist view (of free will and determinism), with a notion of free will which he claims would be compatible with scientific knowledge. The image of reconstructing a ship at sea is inspired by Otto Neurath, when he argued against the existence of pure protocol sentences in *Erkenntnis* III (Leipzig: Meiner, 1932) and in A. J. Ayer, *Logical Positivism* (Glencoe, IL: Free Press, 1959).

From Now On: playing and imagining God

p. 85 The comparison of human projects with cities by Benjamin Disraeli comes from his novel *Coningsby, or the New Generation* (London: Longmans Green, 1844); I came across this reference in Freeman Dyson, *Infinite in All Directions* (New York: Harper & Row, 1988), pp. 37f. John Brooke and Geoffrey Cantor in their book *Reconstructing Nature: The Engagement of Science and Religion* (Edinburgh: T & T Clark, 1998) devote the tenth chapter to ambitions to 'improve nature'. They observe that chemistry is conspicuously absent from the scientific disciplines that are at the heart of 'natural theology', attempts to argue from the way the world is to God as its maker.

p. 86 A. D. White, *A History of the Warfare of Science with Theology in Christendom*, 2 vols (New York: Appleton, 1896). Frederick Ferré, *Hellfire and Lightning Rods: Liberating Science, Technology, and Religion* (Maryknoll, NY: Orbis Books, 1993), 27.

p. 86 On insecurity behind the call 'not to play God' there is an interesting essay by Ronald Dworkin in *Prospect Magazine* of May 1999.

pp. 86–88 The U-shaped profile summary of the Bible comes from Northrop Frye, *The Great Code* (San Diego: Harcourt Brace Jovanovich, 1982), p. 169; see also S. Terrien, *The Elusive Presence*. 'Co-creator' is a term used on various occasions by Philip Hefner (*The Human Factor*) as well as others. My first explorations on 'transformation' as a central theme were in *Beyond the Big Bang*, pp. 150–154. The expression 'to god the world' has been inspired by Isabel Carter Heyward, *The Redemption of God* (Lanham, MD: University Press of America, 1982).

pp. 89–90 On my hesitations regarding a scientific or naturalistic replacement for the plurality of traditions, rather than a reinterpretation of traditions with an open attitude towards others, see *Zygon* 33 (December 1998), pp. 617–633. *Everybody's Story: Wising Up to the Epic of Evolution* is the title of a book by Loyal Rue (Albany, NY: SUNY, 2000)

pp. 90–92 Gerd Theissen, *Biblical Faith*. See on extraterrestrials S. J. Dick, *Plurality of Worlds* and *The Biological Universe* and M. J. Crowe, *The Idea of a Plurality of Worlds*. This section was previously published as 'Betlehem: Center of the Universe?' in Russell Stannard (ed.) *God for the 21st Century* (Philadelphia: Templeton Foundation Press, 2000).

p. 96 John Fowles, *The Aristos*, rev. edn (Falmouth: Granada, 1981), p. 19.

Index